NEAR MISS

Bobby Lee Martinez

NEAR MISS

Copyright © 2019 by Bobby Lee Martinez

All rights reserved. No part of this book may be used or reproduced by any means, graphic, electronic, or mechanical, including photocopying, recording, taping, or by any information storage retrieval system without the written permission of the publisher except in the case of brief quotations embodied in critical articles and reviews.

ISBN: 978-0-9965785-3-0
ISBN: 0-9965785-3-6
Library of Congress Control Number: 2018963366

Cover and text design: Miko Radcliffe

Sacred Life Publishers™
SacredLife.com
Printed in the United States of America

For my Canine Companions who walk with me on this spiritual journey of understanding my relationship with the visitors. And a special thank-you to Richard Fisher for his computer skills; Cindy Narayan, who listened to this story a long time ago and is now a witness; and Sharon Lund, whose support and guidance is unwavering.

Contents

Dedication iii

Preface vii

Introduction ix

1   A Secret Place 1

2   Sightings: Harbinger of Earth's Cleansing 9

3   Surviving an Unfamiliar Planet 17

4   Sombra: The Next Step in Mutant Transformation 23

5   Spotlight on Bishop's Lodge Road 31

6   SHIKARI 39

7   A Dire Warning 49

8   The Beckoning Voice 57

9   Twilight with "The Dark Force" 63

10 Archetypes! 69

11 Krystela 77

12 Alien Visitor or Messenger? 87

13 Earth Begins its Restoration 93

14 Mutants: "Evolved Beings" 103

15 Extraterrestrial Visits 111

16 "Companion" and Missing Time 131

17 Star Child 141
18 The Return 149
19 The Mission 159

Preface

This account is more than science fiction. It is a narrative woven around the real events that eyewitnesses, myself included, say are happening now, and have been happening for many years, to select human beings on our planet. Many of the recipients of these events have formed support groups for themselves as unwilling victims of alien abductions and, as a result, have become an unofficial cadre of investigators of UFO activity.

At the same time, the military arm of the United States and those of other foreign governments continually deny that UFO phenomena exist. Be that as it may, based on reports from around the world, a large percentage of the world's population is estimated to have had some form of contact with UFOs or UFO-related activity.

In this account, Adan, Sombra, and Daisy represent real beings who lived through the many incidents described in the story—either through dreams, remembered past lives, channeled information, or direct conscious-waking experiences. For those who have become believers, no explanation is necessary. For the skeptics, no explanation holds true.

Unexplained sightings of UFOs, interaction with alien beings, missing time, and asteroidal near miss phenomena serve as the core events from which this unique story unfolds.

Introduction

Detected by astronomers only four days before, an asteroid called 1996 JA-1, about a third of a mile across, whizzed by the Earth at approximately 10:48 a.m. mountain standard time on May 18, 1996, in a dramatic near miss. This asteroid, the largest ever observed in recorded history, up until this event, missed Earth by approximately 279,000 miles, at a speed of approximately 10 miles per second — a "near miss" in astronomical terms.

This asteroid came closer to the Earth than all but five other detected asteroids and was one-tenth the diameter of the one believed to have impacted Earth 65 million years ago, causing the extinction of the dinosaurs and most other living beings.

At this time, little is known about any widespread effect this near miss has had on the life processes of our planet. Any correlation to natural phenomena occurring across our planet, at this point in time, is only pure speculation according to scientists who are studying this question at the Los Alamos and Sandia labs in New Mexico. Scientists at these labs have been studying recently discovered changes in the physical properties of energy and matter, at the subatomic level, with reference to near miss phenomena and any correlation among them.

What is theorized is that an impact on the Earth's surface of an object the size of 1996 JA-1 could produce an explosive blast equivalent to 4,000 megatons of TNT. Furthermore, if it were to collide with any landmass, it could leave a crater several miles wide, shrouding Earth in a dust cloud for many years while devastating areas beyond the impact zone for hundreds of miles. On the other hand, landing in the ocean, it could cause towering tidal waves that travel in all directions, engulfing islands and coastlines, as well as far inland. In either case, the results on the global weather patterns would adversely affect every living being on the planet.

At this time, scientists and government officials around the world have consistently asserted that there are no signs of any correlation between the changing of our worldwide environments and asteroidal near miss phenomena in our galaxy—at least that is the "official" word.

1

A Secret Place

"Looking back now," Adan mumbled, "how could we have missed the signs? It began with the near miss of the earth by the asteroid on May sixteenth, nineteen ninety-six . . . the severe global drought that began that spring, the wildfires that destroyed most forests, the flooding, the tornados, the continental shifting, the earthquakes, the volcanos, the progressive rise in temperatures across the . . . "His voice trailed off, his words becoming inaudible.

A picture of the most-frightening sign of all had just intruded his thought: the mutants! The few survivors—first, Sheila, the not so prudish neighbor lady growing an "extra" breast between the other two, and then he, himself, growing an extra ear directly off his left eardrum from within his regular ear giving him two complete ears on that side. He cringed as he relived the pain of that experience.

There were the others worse off than he, with mutations progressing from the body to the mind and spirit and soul as the phenomena moved through the most unfortunate of the population. They had been feared most of all, exhibiting most characteristics of the zombielike creatures popularized by horror movies.

He remembered the two guys who had lived together next door. Both had been exclusively committed to one another and their jobs. Pappi developed the ability to manipulate people's behaviors around their deepest, darkest feelings. And Ryan developed the uncanny ability to practice on Pappi what Pappi had manipulated. They gave new meaning to the developing chaos of that time, ultimately ending their lives during one of their entanglements. He shuddered as tears rolled down his face over memories long past.

"Why did we disregard the signs? A civilization so technologically advanced, yet so narrow-minded!" he snapped, trying not to think about it. Being a disciplined psychotherapist, he was used to blocking thoughts. He had helped many a client with unwanted thoughts.

Speaking softly and deliberately, he began again. "On the morning of the near miss, I remember waking to the wind rustling through the lilac bushes, the heavy perfume wafting through my open window, and the constant

1—A Secret Place

ringing of the wind chimes outside. Then, between power outages, we listened to assurances on television by our government officials that there was nothing to worry about because the asteroid would be missing the Earth at a distance to be about the same as between the Earth and the Moon!" His tone became harsh. "But what the scientists hadn't counted on was the 'reverse magnetic polar shift.'

"Interestingly, when first proposed to Einstein, years before, he concurred. He theorized the shift to happen in an instant, amid thousand-kilometer-per-hour winds, twenty-story tidal waves, and massive weather disruptions while the actual crust of the Earth slid around its core in the direction of the opposite magnet pole. The shift of magnetic polarity having been accomplished, the land and water would, again, be at rest.

"Tragically, there were two important points that were proved wrong from the original theory. First, no one figured that the magnetic field sliding around the planet would result in the physical mutation of its inhabitants. Second, it never occurred to anyone to think about the effects on their nonphysical realities, such as thought processes, feelings, spirituality, relationships, or psychic experience. Science was so myopic at the time, concentrating only on the physical effects of Earth. And maybe because no one, not any living thing, was supposed to survive . . . " he said sadly, trailing off to a whisper as if waiting for a response.

He suddenly realized that all this time he had been talking aloud to himself. A cold, suffocating nostalgia began to well up inside him and seemed to wrap around him like a noose. The realization seemed to startle him time and time again.

"Strange that I still react that way," he said. "I haven't spoken to another human being since the violent civil uprisings by the few survivors and the fall of our government that followed shortly thereafter."

The sequence of events seemed to jumble together: the near miss; the violent changes to Earth; the mutant phenomena in humans, plants, and animals; our government's inadequate response; the riots; and the subsequent fall of all world governments and societal institutions.

"Even you, Sombra, have not been paying much attention to me lately," he whispered and expelled a long, deep sigh. His constant companion of seventeen years, the black, but graying, Pekingese–Chihuahua had been the only expression of life keeping him from complete and total insanity.

And with the advent of Earth's changes, even the few animals that had managed to survive had experienced both physical and psychic mutation also. Some, like Sombra,

1—A Secret Place

developed extraordinary, human-like qualities, exhibiting an accelerated evolutionary process. Others, like some of their human counterparts, became distorted, unrecognizable creatures, reminding him of childhood nightmares and creatures from gothic novels. The same happened to trees, shrubs, and plants.

"I'm sorry, I guess I expect too much of you. I'm only glad you were spared the other types of horrific mutation. I'm only feeling sorry for myself right now. It's just these thoughts."

Sombra lifted his head and nodded in agreement. He had been napping. Although Sombra could not talk, he was developing the ability to communicate with a series of gestures and vocalized grunts, which Adan attributed to the mutant phenomena both in himself and in his dog.

Adan smiled at his loving companion and told him that he needed to spend more time in his "secret place" to try to figure out the thoughts that, lately, had become so intrusive.

"I need to practice going to that secret place, my secret place inside, to find answers . . . to find balance . . . to keep the overwhelming present from taking over my memory and robbing us of our future, like it did to everyone else," he said firmly.

Daily he would repeat going to that secret place in his mind through his feelings. Calling the practice his *remembering session*, he found that he could relive his past experiences with extraordinary detail and emotion. He also began to recognize that he actually entered the past through his own feelings and memory processes. And while there, he focused on learning any new details. He always sought any clue in the past that could have led to this present. Then, upon returning, he would share them aloud with Sombra, developing new insights into their experience. And when sharing his insights with the few other survivors that happened by, they only talked of the past as a dreamlike intrusion on their "immediate moment living" and then shunned him for reminding them. That is why he called his remembering experience his "secret place."

Over time, all but Adan lost even those vague intrusions. Life, very quickly, had become a wasteland of lost souls wandering aimlessly while struggling to survive. He hoped it was Earth healing its inhabitants as a preparation for a new birth, but he wasn't so sure. It was, more likely, the logical outcome of a race that never learned lessons from its past when preparing for its future.

"That is why I must continue journeying to that secret place—to remember, to learn, and to prepare—finding purpose in this strange new world, with you, Sombra, by my side."

2

Sightings: Harbinger of Earth's Cleansing

"Oh—my—gosh, Sombra! What could this mean?" he exclaimed. This morning, as he had journeyed to this secret place, he was overwhelmed by evidence of a subtler sign that had been with him since childhood. It was the phenomena of the sightings! UFO sightings! He was shocked as he began recognizing that it may have even foreshadowed the arrival of the asteroid and changes to Earth that followed.

"Is that why so many of the UFO sightings, immediately preceding the near miss by the asteroid, left the impression on the observers that some great cataclysm, or disaster, was impending? But why is it that *I* am able to remember when no one else can? And why now?" he yelled. He was becoming extremely agitated.

Startled by the sudden noise, Sombra, seemingly unnerved by his master's disquiet, proceeded to grunt, sit upright, and wave his paw as was his custom when wondering what the problem was.

"It's okay . . . I'll be all right in a moment." He paused, searching for a means to understand this growing consciousness and share it with his inquisitive little friend.

After a moment he said, "You see, Sombra, since I've started to practice remembering, I'm coming to the realization that from as far back in my youth that I can remember and up to the present, I've had experiences with UFOs"—his voice faded, and an eerie chill crawled up his spine as he continued—"and with extraterrestrial visitors."

Those words had a strange familiarity as he heard himself say them. But, clearly, example after example was pouring into his awareness. "What's extraordinary is that, taken as a whole, the experiences of those select individuals who have had UFO experiences point to a preparation. And in my opinion, the most recent examples that I can remember pointed specifically to the near miss and what's followed," he said. "And for me, it's been a very personal and lifelong preparation because I can remember! Oh boy, this is too much to grasp." He felt overwhelmed by the thought.

Sombra then proceeded to get down on all fours, walk over, and lean on him to give him comfort. Adan realized then that he was getting carried away in the manner of his verbalizations. He often argued aloud with himself as a way of retaining his memories. "Thanks, Sombra." He lifted the dog onto his lap. "You're the only one that I have to listen to me," he said tenderly as Sombra licked his face.

After playing with Sombra for a while, he began to revisit the encounters other individuals and groups had had, with UFOs and extraterrestrial life forms, just prior to the near miss of the asteroid. He felt it was very helpful to keep his past and future memory processes from deteriorating into the apathy of the present he shared with the remaining survivors.

"I remember one of the most recently reported cases, before the asteroid incident, involving Russian children at a day-care center," he said. "Not only did the children report seeing a UFO in the sky, but they also stated that it landed on the playground. And in a bizarre twist, they each described small creatures, with big black eyes, that walked among them and had left them with a foreboding that *something* was going to happen!

"It was clearly a warning, but everyone dismissed the incident as childhood fantasy joined to Russian propaganda." He paused for a moment. "You have to understand that, even after the fall of the communist government, Russia still was not trusted by many other countries, especially by the US," he said dolefully. He was becoming painfully aware of how governmental politics could have influenced the possibility of belief, of this magnitude, by denying it. It seemed almost insidious, yet he believed that that indeed was what had happened.

"But how, and on such a massive global scale, could this have taken place?" he queried. "I could understand authority figures manipulating information, which they all did regularly, especially regarding UFOs. But what about the everyday people of the world? What part did they play in causing this global transformation?" He became pensive for a while before speaking again.

"I believe our part was in the fact that we put all our faith in churches, governments, institutions, and systems outside of ourselves and abandoned listening to our feelings, our hearts, and not acting from them, Sombra. We then externalized everything from our not taking responsibility for our actions to the consequences and the results thereof, which amounted to our failure. And in response to our predicament, we became deaf to our own longings, fearful of what we would find if we listened. Then we failed by choosing not to look inward in a humble and honest appraisal of what we had become . . . haughty, self-centered, insecure, and unfeeling—in a word, heartless. We became totally self-serving, prejudiced, judgmental, and avaricious, jealous, and spiteful of one another, thus avoiding our feelings by becoming totally intellectual, or so we thought. We were only hiding, using intellectualization as a defense for not listening to our hearts.

"This manifested in a number of ways and became most pointed in the worldwide epidemic of divorces and failures in relationships, gay and straight, expressed as issues of power and control. Then came the self-righteous overreaction by right-wing fundamentalists and religious leaders, giving rise to white supremacists and Neo-Nazis in the worldwide movements of populism and nationalism, in the name of family and family values. Time and time again these movements were exposed as nothing more than prejudice and racism against those who refused to give in to fear by not compromising their values and the nondenial of their feelings. We even went as far as electing a corrupt and morally bankrupt person to the presidency who later was removed from office and jailed. We also elected corrupt congressional representatives as an excuse for our failures, so we could have them to blame without having to take any personal responsibility for our failures. Even the young people's massive demonstrations around the world failed to bring about changes in legislation to curb gun violence in our schools.

"Totally ignoring the positive, optimistic steps we could take in healing ourselves, one another, and the planet, that is what happened. But not all of us were that way, mind you. No, some of us were considered radicals and eccentrics because we lived from our connection to our hearts and feelings, choosing not to follow the masses and corrupt authority figures. But those who gave into the aberration of power and control did so all in the name of God, religious practice, patriotism, and societal ideals.

"I also believe that that is why the proliferation of environmentalists, animal rights activists, gays, lesbians and the trans-gendered became a worldwide phenomenon at this time. They became the standard bearers, albeit unconsciously, of what came to be described as the Universal Rights Movement. This became a worldwide movement, born from within the individual, focused on universal human and animal rights, tolerance of diversity, ecological responsibility, and peaceful nonviolence. They bore, in a very personal way and as a group, this symbol of healing for the world community. It was Earth's last gift to the putrefaction of a dying humanity which became manifest throughout the world at this time," he mused.

2—Sightings: Harbinger of Earth's Cleansing

"It was also the sign of an opportunity which could have saved our world without the cosmos having to intervene on its own terms. Taken in total, that was the sign: subtle yet so obvious and blatant." He remembered the very wise phrase about looking inward to the heart and discerning an outward experience: "For those who have eyes to see, ears to hear . . . ."

"You know, Sombra, I believe the asteroid was just an excuse for Earth to cleanse itself and create a balance around what we had forgotten—our feelings from our hearts—our everyday, run-of-the-mill subtle feelings of heartfelt compassion for one another, like the examples of the lives of Mother Teresa, Gandhi, and the Dalai Lama," he said.

Sombra seemed to agree as he curled up in a little ball and proceeded to fall asleep.

After a rest period that lasted for several hours, other examples came to Adan's mind as the wind whistled around him and Sombra. As he dissected each incident, he became thoroughly convinced of the message brought by the *Visitors*, which warned of what had been the upcoming global events and the need to prepare for them by exercising feelings of heartfelt compassion. In retrospect, he felt badly that only a few people around the world had recognized and discerned the signs.

He also believed that his personal preparation had something to do with the present and future, following the Earth's changes. This much he knew. But, because of the trauma of having lived through the chaos, he would have to revisit each of his visitations by the extraterrestrials to rediscover his role in the creating this future world with his faithful friend at his side. After all, Sombra had been involved in the last seventeen years of his preparation and had lived through this chaos with better success than he. Somehow, Sombra seemed almost a necessary part of this cosmic plan unfolding before them.

3

Surviving an Unfamiliar Planet

Processing the insights of his last *remembering session* had taken a week, as he had been distracted by some unfamiliar weather phenomena. And today was a particularly gloomy day. Storm clouds had completely covered the sun for the first time in months. He felt enveloped in an eerie stillness interrupted only once in a while by the rumblings of thunder and flashes of light, presumed to be lightning. He never knew for sure since Earth continued to struggle to find its balance.

"Mind you, I'm not complaining," he said. "After all, the sun isn't blazing down on us, Sombra. But still, I'm afraid of what might fall from the clouds." It had not rained in months since the asteroid incident. "You know it may not even be water that falls from the clouds, even though it may be essential for the cleansing process, no matter how toxic." Both shuddered at the prospect, even as they enjoyed the reprieve from the unmerciful heat.

He had been quite surprised by the swiftness at which the changes to Earth had taken place and the months it was taking for Earth to recover. As for the population, so few survivors could be considered as such. Most had died in the early days of the violent changes following the asteroid's near miss or in the societal upheavals that happened afterward or because of the severe drought and difficulty of life they had moved away. Eventually, survivors became mutants like him and continued mutating until they would either succumb to strange diseases associated with their mutations or accept what they had become. The *others*, outliving most survivors, continued to mutate and became unimaginably violent as they preyed on any unfortunate creature that had the misfortune to cross their path. They added a new dimension of horror to a postapocalyptic world.

"Sombra, let's take advantage of the cooler temperature and go exploring before my memory session, unless it starts to rain."

Lately, they had spent most of their time indoors in makeshift living quarters in one of the department stores in one of the local shopping malls in Santa Fe. Once as icons of modern society, the malls had been abandoned after the

3—Surviving an Unfamiliar Planet

rioting and the demise of the population that left entire towns like Los Alamos and Espanola empty. Vacant homes and buildings now stood as if in silent testimony to a passing humanity. Only some villages and the Indian pueblos had remained somewhat populated. For him and his dog, the interior rooms of the mall provided necessary protection from the severe heat and cold, as well as safety from the unsavory human and environmental elements around them. Surprisingly, necessary food was also plentiful from the storerooms of its grocery stores and food shops.

At that moment it began to rain. Peering through a plate-glass window, he shouted, "Look, Sombra! The rain is burning through the refuse in the parking lot." It really wasn't burning, as such. It was more like smoldering until the objects became a runny ooze that partially disappeared in clouds of smoke. They could even hear the objects sizzle.

Sombra stood on his hind legs and looked intently at the amazingly bizarre sight. Pieces of paper, cardboard boxes, dried-up leaves and weeds, and even the fabric of the tops of the automobiles seemed to wilt, crinkle, and melt under the falling "rain."

"Aren't you glad we didn't go out there, Sombra? But we do need to monitor the 'rainfall' until it's safe," he said coolly. "In the meantime, let's check out the ceilings in this building and hope that they'll hold up long enough to outlast this latest cleansing by Mother Nature."

At that moment a scary thought crossed his mind. "Sombra, let's go to the sporting goods store and find the gas masks we saw in the display case a few weeks ago. You never know what kind of toxic gas is being produced by that rainfall," he cautioned.

They hurried through the debris of the mall while glancing up at the ceiling in the hope of not finding the telltale cloud of dripping ooze. They were lucky, this time, he thought.

Ordinarily, he had thought of himself as an optimistic and hopeful person. For years he had struggled with reticent clients who were so laden with psychological problems that they became a real challenge for his own personal optimism. He had often joked that when it came to being optimistic, he likened himself to a dentist—always pulling teeth, in his case, optimism, out of his clients, even in the direst of circumstances. He was now practicing on himself.

He remembered some women in his practice, like Cindi and Rapiddy, who would sometimes gently kick him and scream and throw cushions at him as he gently nudged them into being more optimistic about their efforts to grow. In particular, he remembered one woman who responded

3—Surviving an Unfamiliar Planet

to the question, "Whoever promised you a rose garden?" by exclaiming in a shrill voice, "You did!" He chuckled aloud. He was pleased with the ease at which he was becoming able to recall things from his past, even if they didn't seem to be too closely connected to the task at hand. He also liked that he hadn't lost his sense of humor.

"Here we are, Sombra. Try this one on," he said. "We might need to adjust it a little bit." He laughed at the sight. From that moment on, both carried backpacks with emergency supplies, including two gas masks and rechargeable oxygen tanks. "See, if we weren't optimistic, with a sense of humor, we would have given up a long time ago and never come up with such ingenious ways to survive."

Sombra nodded and began to make whistle like noises, to Adan's astonishment, as if trying to relieve anxiety. Slowly they made their way back to their living quarters while the gaseous clouds and noises outside provided an uncanny backdrop to an already-tense living situation.

4

Sombra:
The Next Step in Mutant Transformation

"As I sit here remembering, I'm confused Sombra. I keep going back to that one incident that seemed to start it all for me. I then consult my journals to find a pattern that will reveal a purpose for us surviving, and I get nothing! Nothing at all! I need to get a hint as to which incidents were related, that I may remember for this future, our future, for our survival today! Or could it all have been just dreams, products of an overactive imagination and a weary mind?" Doubting, he was pleading with himself. This was strange behavior for him; he never doubted himself.

Sombra then did a curious thing. It was a combination of gestures and a series of grunts. Then he fell to the floor and began pushing the journals to one side while clutching his chest in what appeared to be excruciating pain. Any effort at trying to help him was met by fierce rejection followed by a repeat performance. He obviously was trying to communicate an answer to his not-too-quick companion.

Finally, the gestures and grunts began to make sense. "What a dummy I am, Sombra!" he remarked, as Sombra collapsed in exhaustion, but with a knowing grin on his face. "You want me to quit looking outside of myself, as in the journal entries, for the answer? I should listen to my feelings through the remembering, and that will lead me to the answer no matter how difficult and painful?"

He paused for a few moments and continued as if a light bulb had lit up over his head. "I see. Each incident will lead me through a series of feelings pointing to a perspective regarding our part in re-creating the future, which, in turn, will give us more feelings that will guide us in defining our role. Damn! I was making the same mistake that led to everyone else's demise. Now that's a scary thought." He shuddered. "See how easy it is for us humans to forget, Sombra? Thanks. I'm beginning to see why you're with me."

"You bring me back to the basic spiritual principle of looking inside and not outside for answers and using my inner feelings for guidance."

He, then, began to reflect on how Sombra's role in his life had begun to take a new turn in the shaping of their

4—Sombra: The Next Step in Mutant Transformation

understanding of this future world. Sombra was now more than a dog, he thought. Yet, for him, Sombra had always been more than "just a dog."

His constant companion, Sombra had even attended graduate school with Adan, at Highland's University in Las Vegas, as he trained for his master's degree in counseling. He remembered how his professors and classmates once commented negatively on how anti-social he was because he would disappear for the breaks during classes. He replied by explaining how he needed to check on Sombra, who would be sleeping in the car parked underneath the big shady trees outside the classroom. So his professors and classmates had then entreated him to bring Sombra to class. As a result, Sombra began to sit intently underneath his desk for each class period from that day forward. He even remembered the head of the counseling department making the comment during the graduation ceremony that the degree should be awarded to Sombra, for being the better-behaved student.

He also recalled how Sombra had been born on the same date as his maternal grandmother, Margaret, under the astrological sign of Libra, the sign of power and justice. That coincidence held a special significance for him. Adan had been very close to her. He often thought it was as if that part of her that had embodied her strength and wisdom had waited to be passed on when she was close to death. He believed that very expression of her presence had become embodied at his side in Sombra, at her death, to act as a type of guide for him as a sign that she was very much with him. Sombra even used the same gestures as she had.

Named by Aurora, Adan's mother, that was Sombra, whose name meant "shadow." And that is precisely what Sombra became for him, the reflection of the subtle, but constant, reminder of the need to use his inner feelings as his guide. He learned his guidance was then to be used in the exercise of the power of the psyche in attaining wisdom. In his personal life, he had followed and lived this truth, and it came to be what he had tried to teach his clients through his relationship with his dog.

And even as a puppy, Sombra showed a surprising precociousness. By himself, he had learned to sit upright on his hind end when he wanted attention or food, to communicate, or just to listen in on conversations. He had even learned to do the popular 1980s' "moonwalk" dance step, or at least his version of it, by watching his nephews and nieces, Dan, Rosalie, Nettie, Christina, and Alicia as they practiced the steps. Sombra would even surprise the neighborhood cats who had strayed into his territory by running and climbing onto the first tree branches as he chased them into the trees of the yard.

4—Sombra: The Next Step in Mutant Transformation

Adan felt an overwhelming emotion as he recalled Sombra's characteristic behaviors but even more so as his mind flooded with examples of Sombra's affectionate nature. For no other reason than pure love did Sombra act to protect him, vie for his attention, lean up against him, jump onto his lap, and lick his face and constantly want to be with him by following beside him everywhere. Even now, these new expressions of guidance and direction he brought forth are a new level of communication based on love.

"Sombra, I believe this is a historic moment. I think that I am witnessing a jump in consciousness, the next step in the evolutionary process, of . . ."—he paused at the mere thought of what he was to say next—"*of your kind.*" He wondered if this could possibly be happening in other parts of the world to other dog survivors.

He remembered the phenomenon of the "Hundredth Monkey Effect" described in psychology. This was an occurrence whereby one member of a species exhibits new learning and the other members of a species, who are far removed from that individual and the stimulus for this behavior, begin to exhibit the same behavior for no apparent reason at the same time. He was amazed at the privilege afforded him. In all his years as a psychotherapist, having observed behavior of all types, he had never witnessed something so remarkable.

"You amaze me, Sombra! What if your so-called mutancy is being assimilated into Earth's changes as part of this new world's evolutionary process? But I do hope that I haven't modeled too many bad habits for you. After all, it seems that your time with me has been used as a kind of internship on which Mother Earth has now impressed a type of consciousness."

He began thinking of the future and the new world that both were being prepared to enter—an emotional future full of feelings of mutual love and compassion, of warmth and acceptance. But thus far, only him and Sombra, that he knew of, had made it easy to imagine. Yet a tangible world, full of mystery and awe, was still unfolding before them.

And how were they to combine the "emotional" world with the "tangible" evolving world that was, as yet, unknown to them? He decided he would begin by teaching Sombra to communicate in the specialized sign language developed for apes and chimpanzees like the one he remembered used by Koko the gorilla. All the information he needed would be in the old library because using the Internet was no longer possible. Hopefully both he and

4—Sombra: The Next Step in Mutant Transformation

Sombra would be open enough to recognize the next steps they needed to take when it was revealed to them.

Also, he felt satisfied that maybe his UFO experiences and *visitation* phenomena would help provide them with answers and the guidance regarding how they both fit into this spectacular mosaic unfolding before them. He thought that he must take Sombra's advice and allow his innermost feelings lead him to the answers. At least that is what he hoped as he looked at Sombra and said, "School starts tomorrow!"

5

Spotlight on Bishop's Lodge Road

"Huh? Ahhh. Oh. Sombra?" he said, yawning and making a smacking noise with his mouth. He loved to exaggerate that smacking noise after a yawn. Sombra was sitting up on his hind end and tapping him on the chest to wake him.

"What's the matter? Is everything okay?"

Adan could barely muster enough energy to gather his wits. Since the asteroid incident, he had gotten used to waking quickly and having to act keenly when facing threatening situations.

Sombra motioned for him to follow, and they both ran down the corridors of their makeshift living quarters. He could barely keep up as Sombra dashed through the mall and out the taped-up double glass doors of the breezeway. They came to a standstill just outside, and Sombra stood fast and pointed to the western quadrant of the sky.

"I almost don't believe my eyes. But how can that be? It just can't be missing—I mean, just part of it like that—can it, Sombra? I'm . . . ." He could not describe the feeling that went through him at that moment. Incredulously as he looked up into the sky, he found that part of it was missing.

Sombra seemed as shaken; he just sat on his hind end, pointing and staring, silent and immobile. It was an awesome sight. It looked as though someone had sliced a wedge-shaped piece of the sky, as one would a cantaloupe, and taken it, leaving the rest in place.

"Two forty-five-degree angles at a distance of elbow to elbow from the horizon, arching upward and meeting in a point at an altitude three-quarters of the way into the sky up from the horizon"—he paused—"but what's fascinating is the contrast between the bright, blue sunlit sky and the dark, black moonlit space.

"But we're able to see the moon and the stars . . . and the blackness of space, for that matter. I mean, I guess there's still a little bit of atmosphere that enables us to see the light and dark together . . . side by side . . . I mean, at the same time!"

Adan knew that he was beginning to blather on because of the mounting fear and anxiety over this new atmospheric development, but he couldn't help himself. So they spent the rest of the morning just standing there,

5 — Spotlight on Bishop's Lodge Road

staring in silence and trying not to think of what this meant for the planet — for them.

Later that morning, after getting used to the missing wedge of sky, they sullenly walked back to the mall. "You know, Sombra, that we must never travel in the direction of the 'sky wedge.' We probably would never survive anyway because I think the oxygen in the atmosphere would become less and less. And I think the air pressure would also become less and less until at the very moment of getting there — *kaboom!* Our bodies would explode at the same time we would run out of air to breathe."

Sombra seemed visibly shaken at the sudden noise.

"Sorry, Sombra. I didn't mean to startle you," he said apologetically as Sombra ran ahead into the quasi-safety of the mall.

Later that afternoon, after rummaging through one of the many storerooms and finding a light-powered camcorder that still worked — a recent invention — Adan prepared for his *remembering session*. Sombra agreed to record each session by turning the unit on and off. Now, he felt ready to begin the journey for the future — their future — by visits to his past.

As Sombra turned the unit on, Adan began to drift backward in time, softly carried on the events of his life. He felt as if he were being pulled by a ball of string being unraveled in the opposite direction. He felt so peaceful now, although the events he was being carried through may not have been so—peaceful—originally.

Slowly, he arrived on a scene that had been etched in his memory so many years ago when he was still yet a child. It was to become the first of many events, throughout his life, that he would remember as actually happening. His heart was racing as he focused on a deserted stretch of mountain road that connected the town of Santa Fe, New Mexico, with his home village of Tesuque. He could not have been more than ten or eleven years old.

It was nighttime, approximately eleven thirty, on a Tuesday in the fall of 1963. He, his father, mother, and one of his mother's brothers had just left the Alley movie theater in Santa Fe. Once in a while, maybe every two weeks after cashing his dad's paycheck, his parents would go watch a Spanish-language double-feature and stay for the bingo game that followed the movies. Only sometimes was Adan allowed to go with them because it was a school night.

"Ricardo, take the back road," his mother directed.

"Okay, Aurora," his father responded mockingly.

Bishop's Lodge Road was a road marked with mystery and folklore in its history that included bouncing balls of fire seen on the mountain ridge, complete with hauntings,

5—Spotlight on Bishop's Lodge Road

witches, and ghosts. It was a road very few people would drive late at night unless they lived in that section of the village or had an emergency and had to use the road to get help, even though it had been the original road between Santa Fe and Tesuque.

On this particular night, the sky was clear and the air was crisp and little Adan felt very safe sitting in the backseat of their blue-and-white 1956 Chevy Bel Air beside his uncle John Isabelito. Through the rear window, with his head tilted backward, he watched the moon and stars twinkle overhead as the car topped the first hill and began its descent into the valley.

Suddenly, the sky and surrounding hills and arroyos, the road, the pinon and juniper trees, and the entire inside of the car were bathed in a pulsating white light. Startled, he tilted his head forward and was surprised he could see clearly his parents' faces alternately reflecting the light coming in from the outside as the car came to an abrupt stop. The light source seemed to be located directly to the right of the car, beyond the deep ravine on the hilltop, not more than 150 feet away.

His mother remarked that the light source was, probably, just a spotlight, calling attention to a movie star function at the Bishop's Lodge resort, located just ahead after a bend in the road behind the hill. Adan was quick to point out that the "spotlight" was not moving across the sky—only pulsating from atop the hill! No one could respond to him with any further explanation.

After watching for a few minutes, he noticed that two other cars joined them, one parking in front of them and one behind. The cars shone brightly to the pulsing artificial daylight. It was so bright outside that Adan could see the occupants of both cars, who appeared seemingly perplexed by what they also were witnessing. As they caught sight of him, they began shrugging and pointing at the light source.

His uncle remarked on how he would like to get out of the car and take a closer look. Although his parents said nothing, Adan protested vehemently to his uncle's suggestion, feeling afraid and concerned for his safety. His uncle only called him chicken and got out of the car.

Then, suddenly, at that very moment, the pulsating light slowly lifted off the hill. It then shot upward into the night sky in a slightly southern direction toward Santa Fe, behind them. Adan watched intently until it was but a dot among the stars and hadn't noticed his uncle's quick retreat back into the car. In silence, his father proceeded to drive them home, while his uncle teased him quietly about being afraid. But little Adan didn't care because he felt he knew better. His uncle had been just as startled.

5 — Spotlight on Bishop's Lodge Road

The visitation was over. Slowly, Adan began to drift forward in time, softly carried through the same events that had taken him back to that first encounter. He believed that he had witnessed and relived the entire scene as a spectator, from a vantage point that had allowed him to witness an overview of the scene, as well as the details, as it unfolded. All the while, he was experiencing it in the present, through the eyes of a child in the past. It was a profound and insightful experience he thought, as he "arrived" in the present.

"You know, Sombra, the feelings I got as I relived that first encounter were surprise, awe, fascination, and fear. But at no time did I feel the kind of fear that told me not to go forward. On the contrary, it was a genuine fear that invites, entices, and compels with mindfulness," he said as he processed his feelings.

Sombra then turned off the camcorder. He wondered if the machine had captured the entirety of the remembering on the microchip. But more important, he knew that he had listened intently so that he could remember as Adan had described the experience in detail.

Sombra noticed Adan dozing. They would rest now, letting the experience "speak" to them in silence. It had been a full day.

6

SHIKARI

"Sombra . . . wake up! What is that? Do you hear it?" Adan whispered softly as he sat up. Sombra had already made a quick twisting motion with his body and was on his hind legs. His ears perked up as he strained to make out the noise. It seemed to be coming from the middle of the mall — a low, deep humming noise.

"Could it be another human? Or canine companion?" The term *dog* did not seem to fit any longer since his witness of Sombra's rise in consciousness. "Or could it be another life-form?" he mumbled.

Sombra did not respond, only listened and watched as they both caught sight of a shadow that appeared, seemed to glide across the room, then disappeared again beyond the doorway from where they had first seen it. All was quiet again.

At that moment, a hauntingly familiar feeling rushed over him, then quickly ebbed again. Adan shuddered. After pausing for an instant, he and Sombra slowly walked out into the mall to discover the source of the noise and shadow. They looked through every room in the building and even walked the perimeter of the parking lot in the eerie darkness but to no avail.

"I don't understand it, Sombra. All the while we were being careful not to make any noise that could startle anyone or anything," he said. "Unless ... unless maybe there wasn't anyone there, uhh, afterward, when we went looking. Yeah, maybe whatever was in the room was leaving and that's when we saw the shadow and became aware of its presence—as it was leaving."

But no, it was a shadow, not a solid figure, that they had seen through the fragments of starlight making its way to where they slept, accompanied by low humming, like an electronic power source in the distance.

His own explanation surprised him, yet it reminded him of something similar that he could not explain. One thing was certain: it had to do with a memory, something in his past he had to remember—but what? And why did he feel the pull to remember?

Now, he was eager to have his *remembering session*. He and Sombra prepared as before. But this time they could not use the camcorder.

"Damn, Sombra, I was afraid of that. I think the polar shifting of magnetic fields of Earth must have screwed up the polarity that governs the memory in these things. It seems to start—it even captures some images on the screen; it just has become garbled and forgetful." He broke into a profound belly laugh—just like some humans! "Ha, ha, ha," he added. Sombra, too, grinned and made noises that sounded like guttural he, he, he sounds.

Once more he began to drift back, backward in time, softly carried by the events of his life. Again, he felt as if he were being pulled by a ball of string being unraveled in the opposite direction. It was a strange analogy, he thought, but it seemed to fit. He also wondered how it was that he wound up at precisely the memory at which he needed to be. It seemed that more than just his memory was at work—that thought was also growing in his awareness.

This time, he arrived on an eerie scene just outside his bedroom window at the family home when he was a junior in high school. Through the bedroom window, he saw himself getting ready for bed. He could see that his parents were already asleep and, from across the hall, heard them snoring through their open bedroom door. In the next room, Dolores, his younger sister by two years, was talking in her sleep, as was her custom in her younger years. His younger brother, Richard, Jr., in the adjoining bed, was alternately snoring and cursing in his sleep, as was his custom in those days. Adan chuckled, remembering just how much of an adventure it was growing up in this particular household.

Just then, as he turned off the light in his bedroom and had laid his head down on the pillow, he noticed a dark shadow glide across the outside of the northernmost window of his parents' bedroom, dimming the moonlight. He sat up and remembered thinking how strange it was that a cloud should move across the moon, obscuring the shadow of leaves and tree branches on the windowpane that he liked to watch before falling asleep, on such a clear and cloudless night. As he observed, he saw that the shadow seemed to come in through the inverted triangular gap in the drapes where his mother had pinned them together. The shadow was getting larger and taking on a human form as it skirted across his parents' bedroom, crossed the hallway, came into his room, and floated closer to his bedside.

Slowly and gracefully, it approached him until it finally came to rest at his bedside—in the shape of a husky man, a dark shadow without substance. There in the moonlight it stood, hunched over, looking down at him, yet it didn't have a face. Actually, Adan could not make out any features. It was just a dark form, about five feet high with a head, arms, and legs attached to a body, and its shoulders were thrown forward, giving the impression that it was staring down at him.

He remembered that he did not feel scared, at least in the beginning. He was more amazed at what he was experiencing than anything else. In a moment of false bravado, he remembered asking it, aloud, if it wanted him to take it to his leader, then laughing recklessly. But, after a long pause wherein he received no response, he remembered that that was the moment when he really became frightened.

He remembered thinking that he should extend his hand to the being in an effort to feel if it had any substance. But he had decided not to because he already knew the answer—he just thought that he couldn't bear the feeling after confirming what he already knew to be true. He then began pulling the covers over his head with both hands and slowly lay down. Paralyzed with fear, he could not think of anything else that he could do. He also remembered the discomfort of not being able to get to the bathroom that night for fear of passing through the dark form.

Periodically, throughout the night, he would peer through a corner of the covers to see if his silent visitor was still there. It was like living through a nightmare while awake—the dark form just standing there, hunched over, and seeming to stare down at him silently and unmoving. Finally, after watching the visitor for what seemed to be most of the night, he fell asleep, exhausted—more so out of running away from fear inside him than from anything outside.

As Adan watched and relived the memory, he noticed something peculiar about the dark form. It was very subtle, and it happened very quickly, but it seemed to "pulse." He had not remembered that aspect of the dark form when he was growing up—probably because of a combination of his youthful recklessness and fear at the time. And something else—once asleep, it pulsed with a brighter darkness and more often, although the actual pulse was slower.

He also noticed a pulsing of light reflecting from outside his window in unison with the dark form on the inside; both were accompanied by a low hum that also pulsed at the same time, rate, and intensity. It seemed to be coming from a large spherical object of "light" three hundred feet away on the vacant parcel of property, just east of Adan's bedroom. He had not remembered this either when he was growing up.

Adan was puzzled. This had become a strange memory. It was leaving him with more questions than it answered. His attention turned once again to the scene happening before him. The dark form began to move away in the exact opposite direction as it had come, through the hallway and across his parents' bedroom, losing its humanoid form as it moved away from his bedside. It went through the inverted triangular space between the drapes in his parents' room, and he watched it move across the vacant property to the sphere of light. Once there, it disappeared in the light, the hum stopped, and the entire sphere lifted silently from the ground. It quickly gathered speed and disappeared among the stars in the night sky.

As he watched the sky, he began his journey drifting slowly back to the present. Funny, he thought, the sphere of light reminded him of the "spotlight" he had seen with his parents and uncle years before as a child. He wondered if this was that same light, and here it was again, now accompanied by a strange, dark, shape-shifting humanoid form that hummed. He now also remembered his cousin Berlinda once remarking to her mother, Margaret, that she had seen a pulsing light coming from Adan's window in the middle of the night. Her mother responded by saying, "You must have been dreaming," and Berlinda said, "Yeah it was probably one of his alien friends." He was also stunned by this corroborating memory that he had forgotten until now.

Once he arrived in the present, he began to ask Sombra questions. "What could the dark form have been? I suppose you followed my commentary with keen attention?"

Sombra nodded a wholehearted yes.

"Good, I hope you have some thoughts about what you heard because I'm more confused now than before."

Sombra shrugged and grunted.

"Aw, you're too modest, Sombra. You've always been the smart one," he said proudly, "and even more so now than ever!"

After resting for a while, they both sat down to figure out the meaning of the dark figure. Seeing its relationship to that shadow that they had seen leaving their room earlier that dark morning was difficult for them. They discussed some possibilities, but they didn't seem to get anywhere. As they were thinking, Sombra began tinkering with the camcorder, and the picture of Adan on the screen began to flutter. Sombra stopped for a moment and showed it to Adan.

"That's it, Sombra! You're right on track! That's almost exactly how the shadow seemed to pulse. So if we try to describe how both are similar, maybe we can infer function.

But what is it about the shadow that is similar to the picture on the screen?"

Sombra pointed out that the form on the screen and the shadow's form were similar by tracing the outline on the screen and in the air.

"My image, my form, it took my form as it got closer. Sombra! It informed itself around me. Information—that's what it was doing, seeking information."

Sombra nodded in agreement as Adan continued thinking aloud.

"But what kind of mechanism or life-form does that? What kind of thing shape-shifts images by projecting them on itself without considerations of mass and force?"

Sombra continued to point to the camcorder and tap on the screen as the image was fading.

"You're absolutely right. Camcorders, smart cameras, cell phones, smart watches producing images and sound, sandwiched together by . . . holographic computing!"

After a few moments of silence, he screamed, "A kinetic hologram, Sombra!" They both looked at each other as their eyes widened. "I read that Los Alamos laboratory was working on a type of super-holographic information-gathering kinematic automatic-retrieval instrument before the near miss. S-H-I-K-A-R-I," he said, spelling each letter of the acronym. "SHIKARI, we'll call it that—a SHIKARI."

The name also sounded familiar. "I remember now. It's an old East Indian term for a big-game hunter, Sombra, a big-game hunter who was sent to . . . to gather information on me then, on us now! And maybe it shape-shifts what it's been sent to study as a means of retaining its memory by absorbing the entire bank of memories into an imprint of the subject to be played back as a hologram. That's what we caught sight of last night! It came back to check on survivors or to see how we were doing, handling all Earth's changes—you think?"

The explanation helped answer their immediate question, but most important, it gave them a framework in which to examine their experience. Just then Sombra let out a big combination grunt–bark–yelp and began to dance around on his hind legs. Adan joined him in the celebration dance which reminded him of the Skeleton Dance made popular by the 1930s' Walt Disney cartoons, and he kept repeating the word, "SHIKARI," in the accent he had learned from his East Indian classmates in graduate school. Exhausted, they literally fell into a sound sleep.

7

A Dire Warning

A few days later, as they prepared for another *remembering session*, Adan began to tell Sombra about noticeable changes in his memory.

"Sombra, it's as though my past and future were merged and fractured into bits and pieces, and those pieces are now acting as guides for the *remembering sessions*. And now, it's as though I'm able to 'sort of remember' things — more like glimpses of the past that are beginning to break into my consciousness apart from the *remembering sessions*. I'm remembering — like the way I was just before the asteroid incident before everyone else lost their memory completely."

Sombra began signing in reverse. "What's that? You say the reverse inertial polar shift, which caused the camcorder to lose its memory also jumbled up mine?

Everyone's memory? But now, because of the *remembering sessions,* my everyday' memory is improving?"

Sombra now used sign language to communicate with him. "Hmm, it makes sense."

"Let me give you an example? Okay. Lately, I've found myself thinking how maybe some of my visitations and some of my spiritual experiences are interchangeable. And I'm really confused about this. The more I try to decide which is which, the more I think I'm reviving that age-old unanswerable question of which came first: the chicken or the egg. I'm not sure if I was having spiritual experiences, clothed in UFO imagery, or visitations by UFOs, clothed in spiritual imagery."

Sombra responded by making the sign for *one*.

"So you think that I had but one experience but clothed it with the elements of the most prominent framework in my psyche at the time. Hmmm . . . you're a smart one, Sombra. And you're probably right because at the time, according to my earliest childhood journal entries, I seem to be viewing the world from a narrowly traditional Judeo-Christian perspective given to me by my family."

Adan reflected on the meaning of what Sombra had just signed. "But, on the other hand, it's never been that clearly defined. You say that it never is, that it depends on whether it's easiest to learn a particular facet from within

7—A Dire Warning

one context or from another which is in part what governs how it's being perceived?

"Hmmm ... then that learning becomes a stepping-stone to further growth in that particular area or becomes the bridge to another new area that needs defining for the individual. I see, but what about the bits and pieces, the themes? They're hints, echoes of lived experience that I need to follow up on, now, through the *remembering sessions*, not in addition to them? Hmmm ... of course—invitations! I'm beginning to understand.

"So where did you learn all this? From me? By sitting in on all those psychology classes and counseling sessions? Sombra, you're fascinating!"

Adan passed this information through his feelings and agreed with Sombra. He understood how differences in these experiences were perceptual, not necessarily substantial, in nature. This new understanding would help them both define this new world in terms of Adan's *remembering sessions*.

"But could it also mean that Earth is finally beginning to normalize itself?"

Sombra signed, "I'm skeptical."

"What? So you think that we're the ones who have begun to normalize ourselves to match the earth? Okay. I'll have to think about that. But, in the meantime, I want to follow up on the 'spiritual' experiences which have become more prominent now."

That said, Adan began to drift back, backward in time, softly carried by the events of his life. Again, he felt as if he were being pulled by a ball of string being unraveled in the opposite direction.

This time he came upon himself, this time a senior in high school, in his parents' living room, insisting that his uncle John take his bed and that he would sleep on the couch. John was the same uncle who had witnessed the very first encounter of the spotlight on Bishop's Lodge Road years before.

He could see himself lying on the couch and looking at his watch as he slipped it off his wrist and placed it on the coffee table. It was 5 a.m. as he saw himself fall asleep. Then a curious thing happened. Adan felt himself being pulled into the dream that he was watching himself have, and he had the distinct feeling that this was not really a dream but a memory of what had actually taken place and was only being recalled in the dream state, like a memory within a dream.

He found himself atop La Loma de San Pedro, the hill directly behind his childhood home. He had spent many a day hiking that hill and surrounding area with his dogs, Dusty and Shorty, throughout his childhood. He would fix

7—A Dire Warning

a sack lunch and start off early in the morning accompanied by his dogs. After lunch, he would usually take a nap while lying on a cliff ledge, one of the many that he climbed. Then he would return in time to do his chores before dinner.

It was about midmorning, with bright sunlight and high, fluffy white clouds against an azure-blue sky and a cool, soft wind that was blowing. As he stood there staring at the vastness of the panorama, he saw a human form dive headfirst out of the clouds directly in front of him. It wore a white robe and a red ankle-length tunic that was open down the front of its body and gathered at its waist. It seemed to be at an altitude of about forty-five degrees from the horizon and about an eighth of a mile away from him.

The form turned right and flew level for a few seconds, then turned to its left and flew in his direction. As it came closer he could see that it was a male, with olive-colored skin and brown shoulder-length hair. Turning to its left, it flew to a position directly in front of him. Rolling its body to face him, it raised its forearms by bending them at the elbow, the scarred wrists palm forward. It hovered in front of him in a lying position at eye level about two feet away. Its facial expression was urgent as it said in English, "Go tell my people that the end is near!"

Then it continued to fly by him and returned to the cloud in the exact opposite direction completing a rectangular route in the sky. Adan could see his younger self standing in awe, his childhood home down the hill and farther west, La Loma de San Pablo, affectionately referred to as La Loma Pelada, the Pealed Hill, because it was bare of trees and brush.

The dream ended at this point, slowly fading in long, wispy, crinkly lines beginning at the edges and becoming more pronounced as they moved toward the center until all that was left was the younger Adan sleeping on the couch. Watching himself in a dream was fascinating, Adan thought. He could pick up any details that he had missed in the original experience to contextualize and better understand its meaning. But that was the issue. This time, nothing had changed. The dream and the original experience were exactly alike.

Adan then watched himself wake up and take a long look at his watch in surprise. Only thirty minutes had passed. He also heard himself repeating the message, "Go tell my people that the end is near." Then he turned, pulled the quilt over his head, and went back to sleep.

Had he just "seen" Jesus? Was this a dream, a vision, or a memory? Was he just given an urgent message? Adan

7—A Dire Warning

was at a loss as he began to leave that scene and begin his return to the present.

8

The Beckoning Voice

Adan found himself being pulled somewhat differently toward another scene in his journey. This had never happened before. Instead of returning directly, he stopped at a scene where he saw himself, as a freshman in college, entering the chapel of Duns Scotus College in Southfield, Michigan, on Halloween night. He had all but forgotten this particular experience.

As he saw himself approach a pew, he remembered that while at a party early that evening, he had felt compelled to visit the chapel. At first, he did not respond to the feeling, but the urge became irresistible. It kept growing in intensity until it became an urgent voice. It called him throughout the evening until he felt he could resist no longer. Excusing himself from his friends, he walked through the long hallways to the other end of the massive building affectionately known as "The Castle" and into the dark corridor that led to the chapel. All the while, he wondered what this feeling drawing him so insistently could be all about.

Once he was inside, the chapel smelled of years of burned wax mixed with the heavy perfume of incense laden with countless prayers that hung heavy in the air. The dim chapel was lit only by candles at the feet of the many statues that towered in resolute silence. Yet, he felt an overwhelming peace wash over him while the shadows of the statues and the pillars comingled, dancing to the candlelight, which made for an eerie visage.

He began to kneel when he heard someone speak in his head, but it came from the tabernacle high on the altar.

"Don't sit down."

"What?" Adan said, startled, as he stood again quickly.

"Don't sit down."

"But why not?"

"Because you fall asleep when you sit, so remain standing," the voice retorted.

Well, that's true, thought Adan. "But if someone sees me standing, they'll think I'm weird," Adan protested, looking around for anyone who may have been watching or listening. Of course, his Bible teacher was leering at him with one eye closed from another pew.

"That's okay. Remain standing and listen," the voice said. "You are going to go through a great trial. It is going to seem as though I am not with you. But I will be more present to you than I am now, even as you hear me speaking to you.

"Live every day as though it were your last. And remember, I am with you always, until the consummation of the world."

"But . . ." Adan protested out loud, his voice echoing loudly in the cavernous structure.

Before uttering another word, the voice and presence were gone from the tabernacle. It was as if a light switch had been turned off and all that was left was a void with no trace of anything having been there in the first place. Complete emptiness surrounded him like a black hole.

Adan watched himself just stand there in the semidarkness, completely taken aback at what had just transpired. Again, there was no difference between the memory and the original remembering experience that he had just witnessed. A sobering thought crossed his mind: Could these have been real encounters with Jesus Christ?

While studying at this religious college, when he had first experienced this encounter, for a moment he may have believed that to be true. But now as an adult with a mature spirituality and serious education in the psychology of mythology, the mere thought of it made him shudder—especially because years ago, he had left all forms of organized religion, specifically the Roman Catholicism of his youth, which he considered to be corrupt, self-serving, prejudiced, narrow-minded, and completely devoid of any remote association with the Jesus Christ the priests preached. He felt the same about all the other Judeo-Christian and Muslim groups, most especially the Fundamentalist Christian groups.

His intense criticism had been validated over the years by the many scandals involving new-age gurus, rabbis, Protestant ministers, preachers, priests, and bishops with pedophilia, rape, drugs, financial improprieties, wars, and terrorist activities, as well as the many prejudiced and narrow-minded hate decrees he saw published by the different groups, including the Vatican.

The latest example for him had been the ineffectual response of the churches and organized religion to the near miss by the asteroid and subsequent changes to Earth and social upheavals. Publicly, they had explained it all as either God's will or the work of the devil, based on a flawed dualistic worldview. But because most people had come to know better over time and organized religion had become so out of touch with peoples' lives, the religious institutions had crumbled.

8 — The Beckoning Voice

As for Catholicism, in a final act of desperation, while in hiding, the Holy Father and the entire College of Cardinals of the Roman Catholic Church had committed suicide. He remembered his dear friend Patricio, a retired Marine Corps lawyer, laughingly repeating, "They drank the Kool-Aid!" That act had ended the last bastion of religious totalitarianism on the earth, which was only replaced by new forms of power and control.

Adan felt grateful for the opportunity to witness that final validation of his criticism of the religion of his childhood. But he also felt hopeful because this new world was dawning without the interference of the churches, fundamentalist right, or any other organized religious group. Maybe past mistakes associated with religion would now be avoided.

As he was thinking, he felt himself drifting forward again, leaving his younger self to stand alone in the darkness of the chapel. A little sadness came over him because he remembered how it felt to be alone to ponder the meaning of these types of experiences, of growing, and of maturing.

9

Twilight with "The Dark Force"

He now came upon himself as a junior at another Christian college he had transferred to after his freshman year and after he had hitchhiked throughout northern Italy. It was after midnight, and the younger Adan was visiting a first-year student in a dimly lit dorm room. If he hadn't known better, he'd have thought he may have, inadvertently, transported himself to the Middle Ages so ascetic was the setting. The furnishing of the room included a twin bed, a desk, and a chair, and on the wall hung a picture of the very stern-looking archbishop who had just been named to the area.

Adan recognized the archbishop as the same who had caused him such grief, leading to his leaving a ministry position he held for thirteen years after graduation. Furthermore, the same archbishop, a short time later, had resigned in disgrace amid nationwide publicity of a scandal surrounding unresolved questions about his alleged inappropriate sexual relations with underage girls.

As Adan looked on the scene he noticed his younger self catch sight of the archbishop's face in the framed picture, which was grimacing wildly. The younger Adan did not inform his friend about what he was seeing. He just continued talking until his friend interrupted him.

"Hey, Adan, l-l-l-look at the picture!"

"What about it?"

"Well can't you see it?"

"See what?"

"The picture ... of—it's making faces! Why, can't you see it? Look!" his friend shouted, pointing to the picture that continued to distort itself.

"I see it," Adan replied calmly. "As a matter of fact, I've been watching it do that for the past forty-five minutes."

"Well, why hadn't you told me?"

"Because I didn't want to influence you if you hadn't been able to see it."

"Well, I'm afraid. Can it hurt us, if it's evil?" said Michael, who was visibly shaken.

"Not at all! You see, you're a good person, and goodness always protects against evil. You're just afraid because

9—Twilight with "The Dark Force"

we don't have a way to explain this; that's all. Don't think about it. Don't give it any power, and remember that evil has no power when up against goodness."

"Well, aren't you afraid, Adan?"

"Nah, not really; it's just some kind of sign. I only wish I knew what it meant, who sent it, and why us."

Adan watched as his younger self bless his friend by tracing the sign of the cross on Michael's forehead and kissing it. Young Adan then embraced him and bid him good night. No sooner had he left the dorm building and heard the massive metal-and-glass door close and lock automatically behind him then he thought to himself that something was about to happen.

An eerie feeling came over him as he walked out into the night. Everything was wrong, backward he thought. The darkness was oppressive without one star in the sky. He couldn't hear the usual traffic noises from the city streets around the dormitory, nor was there any cricket noise to be heard on the grounds where he walked. Everything seemed turned around. The lamplights, which were normally on, were off. The single light bulb at the tennis court, ordinarily kept off at night, was the only illumination on the grounds.

Young Adan kept walking and crossing himself with a blessing, in Spanish, that his grandmother had taught him, but it was only to be used if all else had failed when confronted by evil. "Alabados sean los dulces nombres de Jesus, Maria, y Jose"—Praised be the sweet names of Jesus, Mary, and Joseph—he kept repeating aloud to himself

He also added, "Why do you keep sending me these weird experiences? I'm tired of dealing with all of these things that don't have any explanations, and no one is being sent to me that has even a hint as to interpreting them for me!"

Adan remembered just how frustrated and tired he was at the time because of the emotional toll these experiences would have on him. He was convinced that some entity was sending the experiences to him. But at that time, the only entity he could conceive of, and blame, was God.

Slowly, he walked across the road separating the two dormitories. As he stepped onto the sidewalk, he heard a rustling in the hedge that ran its full length until the entrance to the courtyard of his dormitory. It seemed to be following his every footfall. If he stopped, the noise stopped. If he took a step backward, the noise followed. The thought even crossed his mind that the noise might be Hortence, the dean's cat.

Please let it be Hortence, he thought.

9—Twilight with "The Dark Force"

He kept walking until he got to the end of the hedge and half turned in the direction of the noise. He bent over slightly, took one more step, and extended his arm. "Hortence?"

He hoped against hope that it was just the cat and nothing else. At that moment, a large, red liquid material shot up and over him for a distance of about twenty feet above the hedge where the noise had been and completely enveloped him.

He screamed like a little girl, raising both arms with his palms out in front of his face in a protective motion. A moment later it disappeared, and young Adan ran into the courtyard, up the back stairwell, unlocked the door to his room, and ran in. He was obviously shaken, and it took him some time to relax before he could get himself ready for bed.

Later, as he closed his eyes in an attempt to sleep, he began to see "gargoyle" human faces that had been slashed and were bleeding. When he opened his eyes, the images would disappear, and when he closed his eyes, they would reappear. Young Adan found that to be very strange and somewhat frightening. Although he didn't understand their meaning for him, he attributed these images in his mind to the shock of the encounter with that red liquidlike substance. He thought that this was, indeed, the most bizarre experience he had had to date and eventually fell asleep.

The next day, the Rector tried to forbid him to tell the story to the other students. He had truly believed young Adan to have had an encounter with the devil, saying, "I have been feeling the devil's presence for the last few days."

Of course, young Adan scoffed at the idea. He did not believe in any type of devil, and he told the Rector that he had already shared the story and that he could not, in good conscience, follow that directive anyway.

Watching his younger self go through this particular experience mesmerized Adan. Yet, he had picked up two extra details that he had not remembered before—feelings of fear and caution and a sense that, somehow, the elements of the experience were a type of projection meant as a warning.

As he thought about it he found himself moving forward again. Slowly, he felt himself leaving the scene and being carried forward through the events of his life. He knew now that he would not return to the present until he had "remembered" each experience that he had framed in the religious terms of that earlier time in which each incident had taken place initially.

10

Archetypes!

Adan now found himself, at a point years later, stopping at a mission church where it was his turn to lead the worship service. It was the middle of the service as he saw himself elevating the chalice cup of wine before sharing it with his fellow congregants.

Suddenly he watched as a two-dimensional image of Jesus seared itself to the inside of the cup filled with wine, accompanied by a hissing sound. He recognized it as the Catholic Sacred Heart of Jesus image of his youth, complete with an exposed heart, two rows of entwined thorns, and a bleeding open wound. He watched as his younger self sloshed the wine around in a futile effort at understanding its origin. His younger self covered and uncovered the cup with his hand, thinking it to be a type of shadow or outline from the stained glass windows behind and above him. He watched himself look around as though maybe it was an odd reflection of a statue in the sanctuary. But it was unexplainable. So he watched himself ponder it until, just as suddenly as it had appeared, it disappeared without a trace, accompanied by the same hissing sound.

Then, slowly, he left that scene and began moving forward again. As he left himself at the altar, he wondered why this scene had gone by so quickly. And again, this scene had happened exactly as it had so many years ago with no extra details to explain its meaning.

He found himself slowing as he moved forward and came to a similar scene at another church. There again, he saw himself amid his fellow congregants, presiding at the worship service. He was witnessing himself at the same moment, like before, of elevating the chalice cup of wine before sharing it.

Then came the familiar hissing sound as the same image of Jesus, in the same form of the Catholic Sacred Heart taught to him in his youth, seared itself again to the inside of the chalice cup. And again, he saw that the younger Adan could not find the means to explain the image as a natural phenomenon, sloshing the wine over the image, covering and uncovering the cup with his hands, and looking around. As he watched the scene unfold, he could not, no matter how hard he tried, discover any extra detail from this scene, no matter how seemingly insignificant it might be if he did find it. The memory of the scene stood firm as it was experienced and remembered — without any means to explain it, once again.

Moving forward again, Adan skimmed silently over the remaining events of his life like stepping-stones on a path to this present and returned to Sombra, who had been waiting patiently.

"Sombra!" he exclaimed. "I'm so glad to see you."

Sombra responded using the sign language Adan had taught him since his rise in consciousness, expressing that he, too, was glad to have him back fully in the present. He then asked Adan if he had acquired any insight regarding the religious experiences and their meaning.

"Well, I hope your insight is better than mine because generally, I didn't gain much. I only sense that they were a type of warning signs about the sacred act of being true to one's heart amid the adversity of daily life. And maybe gaining the strength needed to prepare for the near miss and the changes to Earth all couched in symbolism, like archetypes.

"For example, religious worship might mean the sacredness of daily life, the heart is love or emotion, entwined thorns are pain and difficulties surrounding love, the cup and wine mean taking in life in a deeper way, and Jesus symbolizes being true to oneself. But frankly, I'm surprised that these warnings were directed to me—that's the part I haven't quite figured out, yet.

"Somehow, I think that I was to be a messenger, maybe because I practiced archetypal psychotherapy before the near miss. I don't understand it all too well, but that's what I came back with. I'll need your help, my friend, in connecting all the pieces."

Sombra nodded in agreement and led him to some food and water that he had prepared for him. They both enjoyed a leisurely meal and then continued the discussion.

"But one thing is becoming clearer, Sombra—that the UFO activity and visitor phenomena didn't end with the massive changes to Earth. If our inferences are correct in light of my *remembering sessions,* and I have a feeling that they are, then I believe it is all leading up to something, like a *final message from or* some manifestation of the *Visitors.*"

Sombra nodded his head in agreement and made the signs for *feelings* and *mission.*

"You say that, maybe, our mission in this new world and the UFO visitations leading up to a final manifestation are related?"

Sombra nodded and added the signs for *one* and *same.*

"Now that's an interesting thought. You've gotten pretty good about using your feelings to inform your thoughts and develop your insight, Sombra. And your sign language is perfect."

Both began feeling pretty comfortable and in agreement about the idea of their mission joined to a "final manifestation of the Visitors." This they concluded to be correct based on their feelings. And they began to further agree on key points inferred from their experiences thus far.

To begin with, UFO visitations to Earth had been recorded since the late 1800s, which few people believed to be true and no head of state had publicly acknowledged. Maybe, thought Adan and Sombra, that was why the Visitors never really showed themselves in an unambiguous way to the public—because most people, their governments, and the religious authorities either could not sustain or refused to accept the possible truth of their existence and the message that they might be revealing regarding Earth's future.

Next, Earth had just gone through massive changes, with few survivors whom they knew about, other than himself and Sombra, and those who had moved away—and their fates were unknown. During this time, Sombra had made a leap in evolutionary consciousness and was playing an important role, in his own right, in defining their understanding of this new world and their place in it.

Presently, the *remembering sessions* were playing a significant role in Adan's understanding. He was beginning to realize why, since childhood, he had believed in UFOs. Furthermore, he was realizing the extent to which, all his life, he had been involved in UFO *visitations*. Even the ones couched in religious symbols as archetypes were beginning to find their place within his understanding.

So both felt comfortable in believing it logical to conclude that now would be the time for the *Visitors* to show themselves unequivocally. The *Visitors* needed to explain the purpose of their visits now that Earth had been cleansed and the survivors would be best able to handle that information, without government or religious authority interfering, even though the physical Earth and its inhabitants continued to change and all were still evolving at a rapid rate.

"On a personal level, we must continue to remember that to prepare, that we may be able to sustain the truth which will be revealed to us!" Sombra signed as they prepared for a long nap.

This rest period was necessary for preparing for the many hours it would take to fully comprehend the different components of the archetypal imagery, especially the religious ones, in light of previous *remembering sessions* and the impact on their present living experiences and their future survival. He even remembered that he had written and published a nondenominational study titled "An Archetypal Interpretation of the Gospel of Mark." He was taken aback by having long forgotten that particular memory. Besides, it had been a controversial work and not widely accepted.

11

Krystela

"Are you from another planet?" the little girl said.

"What? Who's there? ... Krystela? ... Ahh!"

Adan awoke with a start. He had been sleeping for quite a while and had fallen off the bed while dreaming. Sombra came rushing to his side and in sign language, asked if he was all right.

"Ohhh. Yeah, I'm okay. I was dreaming. I was a kid with a bunch of other kids in a flying saucer, and this little girl came over to talk to me ... her voice was strangely familiar, and it startled me, but now I can't seem to remember who she was.

Sombra was signing feverishly. "What? You say that I mumbled the name Kystela? Hmmm. That's right. It seemed to be Krystela's voice, and she was asking me if I was from another planet! ... Sombra signed, "I remember her!" What? You remember her? Vaguely? Well, all I remember is that she was a strange woman my cousin was trying really hard to set me up with.

"But why would I dream of her now, so many years later and as a child? You say it might have something to do with understanding our mission and all the remembering I've been doing? And you think I should have a *remembering session* around my past experience of her? Sombra signed, "Do now? Because of her question and the fact that she showed up as part of my UFO stuff? In other words, my psyche is bringing forth another hint for me to follow up on. Okay, if you believe it's that important, because, frankly, I'm not sure either way. By the way, I feel like I've been sleeping for hours. Sombra signed, "sleepy old man, long hair and beard." What? Who are you calling Rip Van Winkle?"

Sombra just smiled. He had read the story in a book at the bookstore while Adan had been sleeping. Amazing, thought Adan.

Adan made himself comfortable right there beside the bed where he had fallen, closed his eyes, and focused his attention. It had become such a familiar experience for him that without much effort at all, he began to drift back, backward in time, softly carried by the events of his life.

11—Krystela

And once again, he felt as if he were being pulled by a ball of string being unraveled in the opposite direction.

Adan came upon himself and Sombra at his maternal grandmother's house that he had purchased from his mother's youngest brother, Uncle Ed, after his grandmother's death. He had remodeled it to suit him and Sombra, and it also had served as his psychotherapy office.

A certain nostalgia came over him, which saddened him, as he remembered the familiar surroundings of their home—the wood stove, the pine hardwood floors, the dark-brown vigas on the ceilings, the pinkish-white painted adobe walls of every room, the white lace curtains over the windows, the enclosed front yard surrounded by rose and lilac bushes, and the fruit trees and vegetable garden. He thought he could even smell the pinon cedar crackling in the wood stove as he watched himself stoke the fire. And there was Sombra in the sunroom, investigating a knock at the front door.

"Hi, 'cuz. I was in the area with my girlfriend when I remembered that I had an appointment to meet with some prospective buyers," his cousin Sylvia said. "So if I can leave her here for about an hour? Besides, I wanted you two to meet each other."

Before he could respond, she had introduced her friend, Kyrstela, a former nun from Canada working as a massage therapist with hobbies that included acting and screenwriting. Then Sylvia was out the door and in her four-wheel-drive Jeep, bounding down the hill on the dirt road at a fevered pitch, running late as usual.

That was Adan's favorite cousin, a real estate broker and entrepreneur. She was a classy, petite, pretty woman in her early fifties, with two adult children, but she had retained a youthful vigor that made her look no older than twenty-nine, with manic energy and a great sense of humor.

"Come in and sit down," Adan said. "May I get you a cup of coffee or tea?"

"Tea, thank you. It is a bit nippy outside," Krystela said. "And I'll just sit down by the stove where it's nice and warm, aye. I got really chilled because the heater isn't working properly in Sylvia's vehicle, and we've been touring all morning."

Adan chuckled to himself quietly.

Young Adan noticed a strange familiarity about Krystela that he could not quite grasp. She was a tall woman of about five feet eleven inches, shapely, pretty, with longish brown hair and big brown eyes. As Kyrstela sat, she began to tell Adan how she had traveled from Canada because she had been attracted to this area of the

11—Krystela

Southwest and felt certain that she had been here before, although she had no conscious recollection.

"This is the Land of Enchantment after all," Adan said with a nervous laugh. "We have everything in this state from ancient Indian pueblos to UFOs—something to enchant everyone."

"Do *you* believe in UFOs?" she queried, in a strangely serious, lowered tone.

Adan was taken aback in mid-chuckle. "Uhh, yeah—I mean, yes. I think I've seen one, actually a few." He had been so surprised by the question and her tone that he responded with more information than he was comfortable in giving to a stranger.

"Well, I've had my share of encounters," she said, "and as a matter of fact, I have an implant . . . right . . . about . . . here." She had begun pressing and feeling the left side of her face in the area between her earlobe and upper jaw with her left hand. "If I can only find it—there, there it is," she said straightforwardly and so matter-of-factly; she didn't so much as wince.

At that very moment, as she pressed in on her jaw, Adan heard the loudest static-type of interference in his ears, as if a radio had been turned on between stations and the volume control set at its highest setting. It was deafening, lasting for as long as Kyrstela had kept her finger pressed against her skin. But he did not let on to her what he had experienced. Instead, for three hours, he alternatively questioned and listened intently about the various alien encounters she had experienced throughout her lifetime. She even startled him by showing him her scarred breasts where she said aliens had made incisions and removed tissue from her.

Stunned, he asked her to alternately press in on the area, once again, where she had felt the implant. And again, he heard the same static interference noise in his own ears. This time, he told her about the static noise he had been hearing each time she pressed in on her jaw.

"I knew it!"

"Knew what?" Adan asked, puzzled.

"I knew from the moment I met you that I have known you from my childhood—like I feel we met on an alien spaceship as children, aye, and like you're a childhood friend I haven't seen in a long time and meet up with you here, now, years later."

"Whoa, okay? Umm, but what does that have to do with me hearing the static interference in my ears when you press in on your jaw?" Adan was skeptical but also smiled inwardly at the thought that this was the best come-on line he had ever heard, not to mention being shown her breasts. And he was also beginning to believe, after hearing

11—Krystela

her recount experience after experience of encounters with extraterrestrial visitors, that she was also intensely paranoid.

But, he thought, it still didn't explain the phenomenon of noise in *his* ears. So could it be that maybe, just maybe, she was not "too crazy" and coming on to him but only describing a reality beyond his own experience? These thoughts were making him feel very uncomfortable; the whole visit was.

"Can't you see," she interrupted his thought, "that the reason you hear the static in your ears when I press in on my implant is that you must have one also? Or at least a receiver! And furthermore, they must be tuned in to each other for a reason, aye."

She was so matter-of-fact, he thought. "Wait! What reason? I just met you not four hours ago!" Adan was agitated by the possibility that he and this strange woman were connected in some way that was way beyond his control.

"I don't know. But it seems to have something to do with my feeling that I've known you from my childhood and that there's a reason for that and for us meeting again, aye. And who knows, but the feeling we may have spent time on the same spaceship together as children, which could explain our connection, aye. They connected us somehow."

"What? Really?" Her logic was unnerving, thought Adan, but it did seem to make some sense, in a very strange sort of way. "Well, if you see them again, you tell them that I want to meet them face-to-face and communicate with them! And I want to remember the encounter."

"Oh, I sure will. Anything else you want me to communicate?"

"No, just that, but I do want to remember the encounter," he repeated as he lost himself in thought about the possibility.

Just then Sylvia arrived with a knock on the door, startling Adan. "Sorry I'm late. These people. I need to get out of this business. You just can't depend on real estate these days. So, have you two gotten to know each other?"

"Oh hi! Yes, we sure have, and we'll have to get together again soon, aye," Kyrstela said, giving Adan a strange, knowing look.

"Uhh, yeah, yes," Adan said, still uneasy from the abrupt shift from his thoughts and distracted by Kyrstela's matter-of-fact, nonchalant attitude, which he found most perturbing.

Krystela then got up off the floor, put on her coat, scribbled her telephone number on a piece of paper, and handed it to Adan as she said goodbye. Sylvia also said goodbye; then she and Kyrstela were bounding off again, in a cloud of dust, down the hill, in Sylvia's four-wheel-drive vehicle and running late for another engagement, as was her custom.

Adan watched his younger self pick his puppy Sombra from off the floor and stand motionless at the doorway. He heard his younger self telling Sombra that he felt an excited unease, as if he were being transported into another dimension of reality, like another eerie *Twilight Zone* episode yet without having time to get his "sea legs" about it all.

He remembered how the phrase referred to first-time sailors who hadn't learned how to adjust their gait with the pitch and roll of a ship in rough seas. Adan and Sombra had spent a vacation on the West Coast responding to the call of the sea. So it was an appropriate comparison, thought Adan. But he also remembered that his feelings were more about familiarity with this new dimension of UFO experience and his acceptance of the information that Kyrstela had provided—and it was his surprising comfort with the whole thing that was the most unnerving for him.

His dream of being a child on a UFO with other children now confirmed by Krystela's feeling about him during the *remembering session* and the fact that he had an implant established by the static interference were now clear examples for him that actual extraterrestrial beings had been involved with him since childhood. This was further proof, and that was comforting yet unnerving.

12

Alien Visitor or Messenger?

While watching his younger self and Sombra, Adan recalled that he had had an additional incident involving Krystela within a month of that first meeting. As he began to remember, the scene at his grandmother's house distorted in a counterclockwise direction and seemed to be sucked into a type of central vortex while being replaced by a new scene. It seemed he was now going to reexperience the additional incident.

He now found himself watching his other self with his cousin Sylvia at Ogelvies' restaurant at First Interstate Plaza on the corner of Marcy Street and Washington Avenue in Santa Fe. Sylvia seemed impatient, which was uncharacteristic of her.

"Oh let's go ahead and order," she said. "Krystela said she would be here and meet us when I talked to her this morning. Anyway, I don't think she would mind if we ordered for—"

"Wait," Adan interrupted. "She just drove up and is backing up into a parking space with her right-rear wheel up on the embankment." He was describing aloud what he was watching unfold in his mind. "She's rushing out of her car; her driver's side window is open; she didn't lock her car door, left her keys in the ignition; and she didn't put any money into the meter."

Sylvia seemed to be caught off-guard, wide-eyed, and incredulous at what she was witnessing, her lips pursed as if ready to continue speaking and her right arm, drink in hand, dangling aimlessly in the air. She continued sitting there, incredulous and silent, as Adan proceeded to describe Krystela's every movement in detail.

"She's coming through the first door to the restaurant; now she's opening the second door."

Both he and Sylvia had their eyes transfixed on the top and bottom edges of the glass door, which could barely be seen behind the wooden screen separating the bar and dining area from the foyer and hostess's station, as it opened abruptly.

"She's pausing for a moment, looking around and turning the corner . . . and . . . here she is!" Adan screamed as a surprised Krystela and an amazed Sylvia looked on.

"How did you know? Forget it; I need another drink," Sylvia said as the scene now changed to a point at the end of the meal when Adan walked, arm in arm with both Sylvia and Krystela on either side, out of the restaurant and up the street.

"So let's play a game. I'll show you where you parked," Adan said, giving Sylvia a knowing look and curious to confirm what he had seen in his mind and described prior to Krystela's arrival before the meal.

"Oh, just up the street, here." He pointed out the old gray Honda hatchback.

"I just hope that I didn't get a ticket," Krystela said.

"Why?" Sylvia asked.

"Well, I didn't put any money into the meter. I was just in such a hurry."

"Oh, we can see that," Adan remarked, gesturing that Sylvia and Krystela should look squarely at the right-rear tire sitting clearly on the embankment. "And you didn't lock your car doors; you left your window open and your keys in the ignition," Adan said tauntingly for his cousin's benefit.

"Of course not; besides, who would want this old thing?" Krystela said, trying to hide her embarrassment at the old car sitting askew in the parking space with her keys forgotten in the ignition in plain sight of the open window.

She then joined Adan in chuckling as Sylvia stared in amazement. Adan knew it had been the implant that allowed him to "see."

The scene began to fade as Adan also remembered that he didn't see Krystela again until shortly after. Suddenly, he made an astonishing connection to a memory that propelled him out from that scene with such force that it made his head spin.

He must have either passed out or come close to it because when he finally was able to gather his wits about him, he found himself in the present, lying on the floor with Sombra alternately licking his face and signing if he was okay.

"Yes, I think I'm okay. Thanks. You're such a good dog, Sombra. I don't know what I'd do without you."

He then began to share his unsettling insight with Sombra. First, there was the fact of Krystela nonchalantly asking him what he wanted her to communicate to the Visitors during their next visitation to her and his response of wanting to meet them face-to-face and communicate with them, as well as to "remember" the visit.

Then, he also remarked to Sombra that no more than six months later he had had a face-to-face encounter with a "Visitor"! Just as he had requested, he had remembered the encounter and even sketched the entity on a page in his notebook!

Sombra signed that he recalled that particular incident.

"But that isn't all of the story. Remember? It also left me with three hours of 'missing time' and no distinct memory of the details of the encounter! And that incident at the house with Krystela and the implant, then at the restaurant—I knew when she was around! I could see her in my mind! Maybe she was either one of them or their messenger communicating via the 'implant'! Or else how could I have 'heard' the static interference or even 'seen' the exact images of Krystela when she was around?

"And what is even stranger is that shortly after having the *extraterrestrial visit* with the three hours of missing time, I seemed to lose that ability to be able to sense when she was around. Then, about a year later when we met for coffee, for what was to be the last time, she confirmed that the *Visitors* had removed the implant at the same time that coincided with me losing that ability to sense when she was present!"

"Strange indeed," signed Sombra. "So she was the messenger for the visit!"

At this point, Adan was weary and breathless with excitement after relating all this information to Sombra. It seemed strange to Adan that this was the first time, in all the years that had passed, he had seen such a clear connection between his *extraterrestrial visit* and Krystela. And he believed Sombra to be invaluable in pondering the information and helping process it by fitting these pieces into a whole picture. Thus, both would be creating a better understanding of their role in this new world that had been thrust upon them because up to now their lives had consisted of little more than surviving.

Sombra listened intently and responded to Adan's agitation by licking his face to help calm him while trying not to minimize the importance of Adan's insight. He signed, "Just rest for now, so later you can have the strength for a *remembering session* to learn the hidden details of the 'missing time' encounter."

"Thanks, Sombra. I love you." An exhausted Adan yawned. He grew progressively calmer as he held Sombra in his arms and nodded off, secure in the warmth of their relationship.

13

Earth Begins its Restoration

For the last two nights, as Adan slept, Sombra had been exploring some peculiar noises which took him into the main areas of the mall. Tonight, it seemed as though Mother Nature was at it again, but this time, there was a crackling noise echoing off the walls with short bursts of light. In fact, thought Sombra, suddenly everything, including himself, seemed to have a magnetic charge. With every burst of life, rainbows of color appeared, surrounding each object in endless auras of multicolored energy.

Beyond the storefront windows to the outside, Sombra could see the magnetic fields of the trees and shrubbery that had managed to survive the years following the changes to Earth. Even the air that filled the space around him glowed in a palate of brilliant pastels while the stars in the night sky danced in a pantheon of infinite iridescence.

It seemed to so beautiful, almost magical, he thought. With every breath, he was filled with the crisp ionization of the very atmosphere around him that caused an invigorating ecstasy. He could feel a power welling up from the earth beneath his paws and slowly rising within him, growing in intensity to a seismic release out of himself and each object in a wondrous unison that made him giddy.

After a while, he could no longer maintain his balance, so he slowly lay down and felt cradled by the remarkable energy that pulsed through his being—keenly aware of all that was transpiring around him. Amid the aroma of freshness wafting around him and the soft crackling and opaque luminescence of the life-force arcing through him, Sombra marveled in awe at this incredible phenomenon.

He soon realized that this awesome display was the restoration of balance to the earth's magnetic field. With each subsequent burst, which lasted longer than the one previous, the earth and its inhabitants regained a balance that built on itself until there was a sustained harmony of smell, sight, sound, and feeling. At its peak, Sombra knew he was witnessing something special that was greater than the sum of his senses. He not only saw and felt it—he was also participating in the display wherein all inhabitants were becoming transformed and incorporated into an invisible but palatable connection between all things and

13—Earth Begins its Restoration

the earth. And he knew that throughout the history of the earth, this connection had come to be described as "Spirit" by a few select individuals. What a privileged revelation, he thought.

Sombra now began to wonder if Adan had been awakened by Mother Earth or if he had slept through it all? He chuckled, thinking about Adan's clumsiness when he felt nervous and how he may have reacted to the activity as he awoke, or had he slept soundly, thinking he dreamed it?

Just then, Sombra heard a familiar sound from around the corner that shattered the peace that he had been experiencing. It was what Adan commonly referred to as "the mating call of the caribou." In reality, Adan was sneezing so hard that, this time, he lost his balance and tumbled into view.

"Are you all right?" Sombra signed, laughing at the sight.

"Oh yes! But allergies? I haven't had allergies since the changes to Earth," Adan retorted. "And I had the most extraordinary dream. It was as if I was in the midst of matter that was alive with colors that danced around and through me. And the smells. . . the smells were incredible—I feel so alive, alive!"

He was beginning to sound like Dr. Frankenstein from an old horror movie. Sombra judged it best to begin to explain, by signing to Adan what had occurred, as he had experienced it. It didn't take long before Adan marveled at Sombra's narrative of his experience.

"So that's what it was—a type of waking dream! But more important, Mother Earth may be restoring her balance—not that I doubt your conclusion for a moment, Sombra. Let's just make a few observations to confirm it."

They decided to test the digital camcorder that had proved useless early on in the *remembering sessions*. This time they would not try reversing the polarity of the batteries in order to compensate for the changed magnetic fields of the planet. If it worked, they also decided to utilize any other battery-operated device to substantiate Somba's theory. But, ultimately, they needed to wait and observe before acting on any conclusions because, under the circumstances, they knew that consistency over time would be the final proof.

"Look, Sombra, it works! It really works!"

Adan grinned thinking of the long-term implications, while Sombra looked intently at the image of himself being replayed on the viewing screen. This is the first time he had ever seen his own mechanically reproduced image and really understood how it came about.

"Fascinating," Sombra signed with a deliberateness that reminded Adan of the Mr. Spock character of the old *Star*

13—Earth Begins its Restoration

Trek television series of his childhood. That particular program, about contact with extraterrestrial life-forms, had been most influential in orienting Adan's thinking about the existence of his Visitors. It also had provided him with a framework for examining the moral issues involved that would inevitably arise as a result of contact.

"You know, Sombra, I've got a queer feeling . . . . We agree that my prior UFO experiences and our survival of the near miss by the asteroid and all the changes to Earth are related, right?"

Sombra, taken aback by Adan's statement, thought that it seemed strangely out of context and signed, "Well, of course we've struggled pretty hard to survive this far and made it to the point of celebrating the earth's beginning to restore balance to herself."

"I don't mean that, exactly. I know it's been a real test of our wits and our sensibilities, and it's paying off—it's just that there may be a negative side to all of this . . ." Adan trailed off in thought.

Sombra looked away from the camcorder and noticed a disturbed visage on his companion, prompting him to sign, "Maybe, in time and through your *remembering sessions*, we'll understand all these types of connection and fill in the blanks."

"My sense is that it's more than just a connection." Adan spoke haltingly as he slumped onto the floor.

Sombra, becoming concerned, sat beside Adan, then placed a paw on his shoulder, and signed, "I don't understand."

Adan paused; then he began petting Sombra. "I wasn't sure if it really happened, so I didn't tell you about it until I was sure. But now . . . more and more, I think it really did!"

"What really did?" signed Sombra.

Adan, wrinkling his brow, began by taking a long deep breath. "Well, the night before last, I was in the middle of a sound sleep, lying on my right side and facing the doorway as I usually do. I, then, began to have a dream that one of those small, dark gray aliens with black almond-shaped eyes and oval heads was pulling me off the bed by my right arm. My left arm was resting lengthwise against my body, and I seemed to be paralyzed as a result of the contact. I also could feel two of its long, bony fingers against my mouth as it pulled me. And I sensed that it was taunting me because of my impotence at defending myself.

"I began to wake, and in that in-between state, realizing that I was helpless against the intruder because of my paralysis, I did the only thing I could to defend myself—I bit down as hard as I could on those two clammy fingers! I could sense sheer shock, amazement, and pain on

13—Earth Begins its Restoration

my impervious intruder, who immediately released me. I was no longer paralyzed, finding myself hanging more than halfway off the bed and partly on the floor."

Sombra, quite reserved to this point as he listened with widened eyes, could not help himself and made a loud chuckling sound.

Adan smiled. "I sat up and called out to you, but you weren't in the room, and neither was the intruder. So I walked out into the corridor and into the main area of the mall. Catching sight of your shadow, by the lantern you were carrying, and satisfied at seeing you were okay, I went back to bed, thinking that somewhere a Visitor would be nursing its wounds."

"Unbelievable," Sombra signed. "I thought the Visitors were friendly and had only our highest good and best interest in mind—at least that's what I believed until now."

"So did I. And do you remember, before this asteroid incident, the proliferation of new-age people and their focus on channeling so-called 'spirit-guides' from other planets?"

Sombra thought for a moment and nodded.

"I think people did a great disservice to themselves by focusing guidance outside of themselves and onto so-called enlightened beings who only spoke 'the truth,' whether or not it could be verified," Adan said, shaking his head in dismay.

"And do you remember how inflexible and intolerant they were if anyone chose to disagree with them? They were like the Fundamentalist Christians, Jews, and Muslims who were once victimized by other groups when in the minority. They, in turn, each became the new oppressors. Each when a majority, lost that interior locus of control most essential for a mature development of the empathic self, which led to the loss of any connection to truth and spirituality. It was similar to those channeling."

"It's no wonder that the world was plunged into chaos," Sombra signed. "It's always one's innocence and ability to see the truth that suffer when one externalizes one's personal power by giving responsibility for it away."

"That's why I believe we must be very careful from now on, Sombra. If the Visitors are for real and are returning, they may have been in the past and could now be nothing more than intruders with their own agenda far different than our own best interest."

"Well, you still have more *remembering sessions* which may enlighten us as to their intentions, good or bad. And we still have the earth and one another," Sombra signed before embracing Adan.

"Thanks, Sombra."

13 — Earth Begins its Restoration

They held each other as they walked out into the emerging sunlight to greet the dawning of a new day with a Mother Earth that was restoring and balancing herself with a potential higher consciousness growing in her inhabitants.

14

Mutants: "Evolved Beings"

The sunlight shone brightly off Sombra's coat as he sauntered in from a scouting expedition to the hills beyond the mall. The air was clearer now and every so often whipped up his ears into two conelike structures, which, along with his upturned tail curling one-and-a-half times and pointing forward on his body, made him look somewhat otherworldly. As he walked, his light-brown eyes glistened with a sparkle that always delighted his companion, who, in the meantime, had been compiling the notes of the previous *remembering sessions* in preparation for the next one. Adan could be seen watching for him through the glass doors of the mall's entrance in case of an emergency.

"Hi, Sombra. How was your expedition?" Adan asked, hugging him and kissing him on the cheek.

"It was great! The air is clear for miles in all directions as far as the eye can see, and the landscape appears to be cleaner than it was before the changes to Earth. But the one conspicuous characteristic is the absence of human or animal life, other than the occasional snake, rodent, or bird," Sombra signed matter-of-factly before they walked to their living quarters.

"Well, I guess it makes sense that if Mother Earth was to initiate a cleansing, that she would use this opportunity to do so on all levels of life on the planet," Adan reasoned as he helped Sombra off with his compact solar-battery-operated radio transmitting and receiving set, one of the few electronic devices they found they could use after all.

"Thank you. And cleansing and restoration may very well be what we've lived through. Yet, isn't it remarkable that the cleansing was so harsh and violent while the restoration was so peaceful and harmonic?" Sombra mused, signing the words.

"And there may well be other animals, or even human life, but not in this area or that may have been in hiding. I'm sure we'll be seeing more mutant life-forms eventually. Besides, what we may see may even be better examples of life, in keeping with the type of restoration we are experiencing in ourselves," Adan pondered as they sat on the futon.

14—Mutants: "Evolved Beings"

Sombra nodded in agreement and with good reason. Both had been keenly aware of their own mutant changes throughout the cleansing and restoration, seeing evolved perception, reasoning, emotional response, and spirituality that continued to manifest as a result.

"Maybe so," Sombra signed, "but what exactly do you mean by 'better'?"

"Well, I've been thinking a lot about that and reflecting on the fact that positive doesn't necessarily mean better. Let me explain. We all know that involvement in negativity leads to even more negativity as a result. There is no possibility that anything positive can result from such a closed system. But being positive and denying the negative is also a closed system that leads to negative consequences as well—behavioral experience has taught that negativity is part of the structure of the positive and, when denied, only serves to ultimately contaminate it.

"What we've been seeing in ourselves and in each other is also 'better, beyond dualism.' It's a balance of the negative and the positive without the denial that leads to confusion and frustration: an actualization leading to genuineness with the ability to be more present. Am I making any sense?"

Sombra, nodding in agreement, signed, "Yes, and it would be nice to experience examples of actualized potential in all types of species without feeling alone, or separate or victimized."

Adan became excited and stood, hardly containing himself. "Of course! That's exactly what I mean! The restoration of the planet signals an era of unity in diversity, a balance and wholeness without the prejudice that results from denial, be it conscious or unconscious. The only thing is that it may be too late for humanity if we are, in fact, only a few survivors." Adan was saddened by the thought.

Sombra saw Adan's sadness. "Maybe so," he signed. "But please, do not be sad, as they all, too, had a choice. Every creature has a choice. And as for us, if we are only a few survivors, we are to be examples of our species. And as such we must remember from what point we have evolved to not repeat the mistakes of the past, whatever the future may bring, be it earthbound or extraterrestrial."

"Yes, I agree. Our remembering must be without agenda or self-interest. That's been in the back of my mind as I've been preparing for the next *remembering session*, which I'd like to do after you've rested for a while."

Just then, both felt a slight vibration and heard a barely audible hum. Their eyes darted from each other to each wall and then the ceiling of their living space and back again. Their eyes slowly followed the vibration hum as it passed over them and continued into the main areas of the mall in a steady southwesterly direction. Without communicating, Adan held Sombra close to him as they followed the vibration hum through the mall.

Stopping short of leaving the building, they looked out of the glass doors and up to the sky. There they could see a lead-colored, solid, rectangular-shaped object that reminded Adan of a section of metal staples used for fastening sheets of paper together. He remarked how the entire section seemed to be composed of individual "slices" just like a section of staples.

They watched, incredulously as the craft moved parallel to them from their right to their left across the sky just above the trees. Then, without slowing, it pivoted forty-five degrees downward from front to back and turned ninety degrees to its left side, reflecting the afternoon sun off the top of the craft as it did so and continued downward in their direction. It quickly disappeared into the foothills just beyond them. With it now being obscured, they wondered if it had landed or just changed direction and altitude.

"The Taos hum," Adan said almost unconsciously.

"The what?" Sombra asked.

"The Taos hum. Don't you remember? It was a phenomenon that was investigated by a government agency and the University of New Mexico in the 1990s that proved inconclusive—at least that's what the official report said. It seems that the entire population of Taos all the way south to Pojoaque and Tesuque Pueblo was complaining of a barely audible vibration hum that was driving everyone crazy. They thought the government was behind it in some kind of mind-control experiment. I even felt it at the northwest corner of my kitchen every time."

"And?" Sombra queried.

"Well, maybe that time the government wasn't involved and they really didn't have a clue. Maybe it was something along the lines of what we just experienced—UFO engine noise, just more of them. And up in those twelve-thousand-foot peaks, who could find them? You see one night after hearing the hum at three a.m., I went outside, and looking up I saw a fleet of parallel streaks of light crossing overhead. It was like watching a radar screen with the blips leaving light trails covering the entire night sky."

Sombra was visibly shaken by the thought of more than one of what they had just experienced—a fleet of UFOs all in one place.

"Should we go investigate or wait until they come for us?" Adan asked sardonically.

"Maybe we should think this through and make a plan with more than two options and then decide," Sombra signed.

"You're right. We need contingency plans for any possibility until we know what we're dealing with."

"As long as our planet's quality of life and the ultimate survival of its species are assured," Sombra signed while looking up at Adan with uncharacteristic concern and an obvious need for reassurance.

Adan suddenly felt cold and could only hold Sombra closer in a tight embrace. "Whatever happens, we will face it together, and I will always love you. And I will always protect you!"

"And I will love and protect you as well."

15

Extraterrestrial Visits

"Don't be afraid. We won't harm you—we'll take care of you."

"Huh? Who are ... Where am ... I? ... Sombra, Sombra! Are you there?" Adan opened his eyes with a start and sat up. He saw Sombra yawning and stretching after a deep sleep. "Sombra, you won't believe what just happened. I mean, I think that I was ... No, I must've been dreaming – I think ... I mean I, really don't know for sure, I guess."

Sombra caressed him with his paws as Adan began to relate what had just happened. "I believe I had a *remembering session* in my sleep about an incident before the near miss.

"Remember before we went to bed? The night was moist. Not sultry, not hot and humid, moist." Weather described like that only made sense after the changes to Earth. "We went to bed after meditating just like we always do—nothing out of the ordinary. I remembered that one night, a month before the near miss, I fell asleep and found myself floating up to the ceiling, between the rafters. Thinking that I would bump my head against the ceiling, I closed my eyes and ended up going right through!

"Opening one eye, I saw myself gliding through the hot crawlspace filled with insulation and up through the roof, arriving in the same prone position at an oval-shaped room covered by a transparent dome. I found myself being pivoted upright, now standing on my own on a flat floor composed of oversized, plain, white square tiles that felt and sounded metallic when stepped on. I was amazed that the entire room and all its contents were completely white in color. The curved walls, light fixtures, countertops, cabinets, flooring; save the clear dome encompassing the room, everything was white!

"As I composed myself I realized I was not alone. Standing shoulder to shoulder with me, two to my left and two to my right, were slender humanoids with black oval eyes in silver-white one-piece outfits. The outfits covered their slight builds from the neck and fingertips to their feet. They were taller than my five feet eleven inches with

15—Extraterrestrial Visits

somewhat oval-shaped heads, small earlike structures, small noses and mouths, and blond hair.

"Looking beyond them, through the clear dome, I could see fluffy white clouds whooshing by against a pale blue, moonlit sky, which gave me the sensation that the room was moving—I guess I believe that I was in a large room within a flying 'craft' of sorts.

"Then the being closest to me, to my immediate left, began to speak to me without moving his lips. I seemed to experience his voice in my mind. 'Don't be afraid, we won't harm you. We'll take care of you.'

"That having been said, I felt myself rotated to a prone position, returned down through the metallic floor, through the roof of the my house through the hot crawlspace, through the ceiling, between the rafters, and back in my bed. I wasn't paralyzed and could speak but didn't. But the most interesting thing is that I don't feel any fear or threat whatsoever. It's as if, on the deepest level of my being, I know we are now being protected—from who, or what, or even why, I'm not really sure. And I'm remembering this in real time, not later!

"But now I do remember being paralyzed when caught by a beam of light that came through my air-conditioning grate in my home a couple months before the near miss. I didn't remember it happening at the time until only days later when I was dancing at the Paramount Club and became frightened when a spotlight came to rest on me on the dance floor. I was so visibly shaken that I ran and hid in a dark corner.

"It then dawned on me that a few nights before that, I had gone to the bathroom at three a.m. and seen a flood of light outside my windows. Thinking my neighbors were having a party, I walked over to the windows to investigate, and I happened to walk underneath the grate. I was then caught by a funnel of light that paralyzed me. I awoke that morning in my bed with no memory of anything that happened until dancing a week later at the club. Strange, isn't it?"

He sighed deeply. "I also remember another incident of paralysis, but this time I was fully awake before, during, and after. It was late evening, and as I began to meditate, I felt a presence was outside my bedroom walking across the front yard. As it entered the yard, my room and every item in it began glowing with a white light, and each item soon began to get wavy as if it was melting, much like when you view a distant panorama on a hot day while walking or driving on hot pavement. And even the light coming from my fixtures glowed differently and bent in wavy patterns.

"I tried to get up to walk to the window but found I could not move or speak. I felt no change in temperature,

15—Extraterrestrial Visits

and my dog at the time slept motionless on the bed and didn't wake or seem to notice. But she also became wavy as did the parts of my body I could see. I could sense the being hesitate at my window, as if looking inside through the glass sliding door, and then slowly walk to the other side of the yard. And as it walked away, my room slowly came back to normal, and I could move again. Going outside, I tried to follow it, but my sense of it was gone, so I returned to my bedroom completely shaken and confused over what had transpired.

"Later on that same evening as I lay reading, four humanoid beings began to materialize to the left of my bedside. They materialized at an angle to fit in my room and were dressed head to boot in one-piece metallic silver uniforms covering their five-foot-five-inch, slightly built bodies. Looking over at them I thought, 'The Power Rangers?' as the second one turning his masked head toward me and nodded; then as he looked forward, they dematerialized. Shaken, I was reminded of transporter scenes in the TV series *Star Trek* while pondering the night's events.

"Later, after speaking with well-respected individuals who study this type of phenomena based on eyewitness accounts, I learned that the being walking through my yard may have been an alien whose hydrogen-based biology causes carbon-based beings to glow, distort, and experience paralysis when in close proximity. Stephen Hawking and other physicists, even NASA, have posited their existence in the galaxy on non-carbon-based planets.

"And I figure the Power Ranger aliens were protectors, tracking those types of encounters and were making sure my dog and I were not harmed, so it was a very short visit. But why would they be interested in us and so unconcerned about being seen while even acknowledging us seeing them by nodding? That is my question.

"And there were even more visits by other different types of aliens, including one that looked like the Ghost of Christmas Future from Dickens's *A Christmas Carol* and one by a Reptilian that looked like a giant insect."

But the most intriguing was the being my Springer Spaniel, Princess Waggles Scheherazade, led me to while we were hiking. It was late summer, and we were hiking up the arroyo by the wooden Canova water trough that my Uncle Ed and I had nearly burned down as children while playing Burn Zozobra. Princess had Cushing's disease yet was still very aware of her surroundings. As we hiked she led me to a fork in the arroyo at a sandy knoll where someone appeared to be firmly propped up against the tree branches four feet off the ground in a cottonwood tree.

15—Extraterrestrial Visits

Nearing the knoll above the fork, I saw her showing a keen curiosity while staring up at a humanlike being; its arms were outstretched, palms and fingers forward; its legs were extended as if it were standing, barefooted; and its head faced forward, its eyes closed. Its form was outlined with feathers, each colored red, navy blue, yellow, and black—reminiscent of a red-tailed hawk except that its torso looked as if completely covered with two feathered wings one overlapping the other. Its head was like that of an older Pueblo Indian man with weathered skin and shiny grayish-black hair cut in a pageboy surrounded by a crimson red bandana and knotted on the side.

I spoke to him repeatedly and received no answer, so we stood there, amazed, for quite a while. After some time we began to leave. He opened his deep, dark eyes; stared a penetrating stare at us; gave us a smile; and vanished. Princess looked around and then to the trees as if surprised at his sudden departure. Astonished by what we had witnessed, we then made our way down the arroyo and back home, with Princess stopping and looking back every so often as if looking for that being.

My beautiful Princess passed away not two months later, leaving me to wonder if she somehow knew he had been sent as a sign that she had been found to be worthy and he was to return for her because she had led me there as if knowing him to be there.

Sombra didn't respond right away, only listened with his head cocked to one side with one ear standing up straight while he stroked Adan with his paw. Then he signed, "So tell me more."

"Well, in the fall before the near miss, early one evening around eight, as I sat reading on my red recliner with my feet up, out of the darkened kitchen in front and on my right appeared a startling sight. Gliding into the doorway was a faceless humanoid shape in a long, tattered black robe with its arms extended out at its sides; it just stood there silent and ominous. After what seemed like an eternity, yet in reality must have been only a few minutes, it silently retreated as if a prop being pulled backward and slowly faded into the darkness of my kitchen.

"Speechless, I stood, and walking into the kitchen I flipped on the light switch, only to find a sink full of dirty dishes and nothing more and the doors leading outside locked from the inside. Another alien, I thought, or an undigested bit of beef, and laughed nervously while mumbling to myself, 'Now I'm seeing ghosts.'

"Oh, and I also remember another dark, moonlit evening while walking my dog, Princess, down the hill from my parents' house. I saw a dark humanoid form

15 — Extraterrestrial Visits

standing silently in the empty, glassless frame of a large picture window of the house next door. I had no flashlight but paused as I watched what seemed to be its Inverness cape coat flapping to the slight breeze. I spoke to it at length, but receiving no response, I invited it to come visit us, and we continued our walk to our home. Upon arriving, I prepared us for bed and after meditating went to bed myself.

"No sooner had I turned off the light when I sensed that same dark humanoid form enter our bedroom and stand at the foot of the bed, silent and serene. I felt a heaviness as its oppressive presence slowly began to overtake, paralyze, and weaken me. I felt no hostility or violent intent from the entity but only sensed that its proximity was the cause of this strange feeling of being drained of my life-force.

"I nicely asked it to please leave and we could meet at a safer distance, out of fear that my dog, sleeping at the foot of the bed and closest to the entity, would be harmed. And it did so promptly. I got up and followed it outside to the front yard to no avail as it had disappeared.

"Again, I researched this type of encounter and concluded that this type of alien embodied a type of biology that utilized a life process akin to photosynthesis but, instead, of light drew on the biomagnetic field energy produced by its proximity to earth creatures, which is most potent at night! Hmm, encounters of this type may have given rise to the mythology regarding vampirism prevalent on our earth over centuries.

"I also learned that NASA, Carl Sagan, and Stephen Hawking all posited that alien life could have a radically different DNA and that Hawking warned that meeting alien life on another planet could possibly infect one with a disease with which one may not have any immunity. But all this happened to me! Here! Now! On this earth! Not some faraway alien planet! They're here! And they have been! Visiting us here! All along! For a long, long, time!"

Pausing and with an inward look in his eyes, Adan took a breath. "And you may not remember, but when you were a puppy and I was teaching you to go outside to pee, we caught sight of a six-foot-tall entity that looked like a praying mantis standing upright behind the coat rack in the plant room. It startled me so badly that I had to pee alongside you! We even slept with the lights on that night." He chuckled, as did Sombra.

"But seriously, I kept seeing those four-foot-tall gray aliens among the tall plants in that same plant room but rarely the 'Reptilians' ever again. And one afternoon as I walked from my consulting room to the sitting room, I caught sight of one gray alien peering out of the archway leading into the plant room to my left. I could see his almond eyes and a thin slit of a mouth; part of his head was angled in such a way that his body was hidden behind the wall, but I could see his long, spindly gray fingers clutching the tiles surrounding the archway.

"I quickly walked back into the consulting room, and as I peered slowly out the doorway to see him, he also peered slowly out at me. I repeated that several times and realized he was mimicking my every action. When I moved my arm, he moved his arm. When I waved my hand, he did his also. This went on for a long time, and when I finally went into the plant room to face him, he disappeared.

"Regarding that visit, I have always believed we were communicating through feelings. We expressed mutual familiarity, acceptance, trust, and a willingness to be open to further connection. At least that is the sense I have had ever since. And you know, since then I can sense when they are around when I feel these feelings in combination, as if they are one feeling, not a series of individual ones, if that makes any sense.

"For example, I remember that same feeling while you and I were moving my friends Robert and James from Santa Fe to Las Cruces. On a particularly desolate stretch of US Fifty-Four adjoining White Sands Missile Base, where the first atomic bomb was detonated, between Corona where the Roswell Incident took place and Tularosa, I got that same feeling.

"We came upon what looked like a stranded motorist. He wore clean white gloves, white coveralls over a white shirt, and white shoes and was bent as he looked under the hood of a white nineteen fifties' Ford truck at a white engine. There were others dressed as he was all in white—some standing, some bending, some facing the road, some facing away, and some standing beside at least two other cars also painted white. But strangely, everything was clean, and no one was moving! Nothing, nada, not a muscle; all were frozen, each holding one position dressed in white and every 'thing' painted completely white!

"You curiously looked out the window while Robert remarked on how he felt badly to see people broken down on such a desolate highway but how he would not stop out of fear, and I said, 'Yes, if they were human!' I then told him of my having had that feeling miles before coming upon that scene and slowed the van to show him that the individuals were not moving.

"Robert panicked and forbade me to stop, warning me that we could have been or could be abducted. I reluctantly agreed and told him of also having a feeling that there was a blimplike craft in the ravine behind the vehicles, as I could also sense its presence surrounded by more visitors, but not clean and not in white, more like a metallic gray craft. So as we drove away, my feeling pointed behind me, then slowly dissipated.

"And speaking of metallic-gray crafts, shortly after that incident, about a week or so later, I saw a traditional metallic-gray disc-shaped UFO in broad daylight. I was leaving my office along with a colleague at about five thirty one evening. She was a nurse who was consulting with me regarding a client; I recall her name was Cindi. As we neared the steps leading to the gate from my office, she grabbed my arm, pointing up to the sky, and yelled, 'Look, up in the sky! What's that?'

"I answered, 'Superman!'

"She said, 'Be serious!'

"'Okay,' I said, 'can you identify it?'

"She said, 'No, but it's saucer-shaped.'

"I asked, 'What's it doing?'

"She said, 'Flying.'

"I said matter-of-factly, 'You've now seen your first unidentified flying object, UFO.'

"She wanted to leave right then, but I asked her to wait as I had a feeling more was about to happen. Just then two chaser jets, one from the south and another from the east, roared into view above us, dispatched, I figured, from

Kirtland and Cannon Air Force bases. They met and trailed the UFO west toward Los Alamos.

"Cindi wanted to leave again, but as I asked her to wait, the UFO returned from the direction of Los Alamos to the point directly in front of us where we had first seen it. It paused momentarily, shot straight up, and disappeared quickly in silence. Then the two fighter jets reappeared from the same direction of Los Alamos and, at the same point, shot straight up in hot pursuit.

"Moments passed when we heard the jet engines pop in a flameout for lack of oxygen, then the whine of the turbines as the engines restarted as both fighter jets came into view again, circled twice and separated, flying away in the direction from which they had come.

"Cindi literally freaked out as she drove away, mumbling incoherently. I then called both air bases, as well as the Santa Fe airport, asking if they had picked up any activity on their radar. They all responded that they had seen nothing of importance and even denied that there were any fighter jets in the vicinity of Los Alamos's restricted airspace. I hung up the phone telling them each in turn, 'I guess it must have been marsh gas!'"

After listening intently, Sombra began to sign some provocative ideas to Adan. "So it seems we have one group of *extraterrestrials* who will protect us from another group of *extraterrestrials,* and both groups may look alike or at the very least are similar in appearance. But, more important, when, or how, did we become so important to both groups? And why are you seeing both groups?"

Adan could only think and wonder aloud about the same thing. "That's right. When or how did we become so important to both groups? And why? I don't know—yet. But I've got a sense that part of the answer will come to light during a *remembering session* about my past experience of seeing that one *Visitor* and those three hours of missing time—at least I hope so."

Sombra nodded as he and Adan began to brainstorm possible scenarios regarding both groups, who now were looked upon, equally, as intruders. No longer were they referred to, naively, as benign Visitors, some good and some evil. They agreed both groups had violated one of the most basic rights inherent to existence in the universe: the universal right to privacy and noninterference. This new perspective on alien visitations to Earth, past and present gave Adan and Sombra new resolve for planning a defense against being victimized.

"What I find strange is that there didn't seem to be much activity or interest in us while the earth was going through its near miss and cleansing," Adan remarked.

"Or we don't have any conscious memory of those instances," Sombra signed, "other than those times when either of us thought something was in the room and we managed to catch sight of a passing shadow or feel a vibration or sense a presence."

"That may be. But what we need now is some way to protect ourselves." Adan bent over slightly; he began pacing and running his hand through his hair, as was his custom when working through a difficulty.

Sombra also began pondering their problem, and for the next few days, all their energy was spent discussing ideas. They finally concluded that although they were unable to keep the intruders from taking them against their will, they would voice their objection and ask for an explanation when given the opportunity. They also determined to struggle against the "victim" mentality—becoming so paranoid that their judgment would become impaired to the point of both becoming worse than the *intruders* themselves. In this way they sought to avoid so many mistakes of humanity that shaped Earth's history before the cleansing, which, ultimately, led to the need for the cleansing.

"I'm comfortable with what we've been able to accomplish, Sombra," Adan announced as they watched

15 — Extraterrestrial Visits

the setting sun create rainbows of brilliant hues in the sky before them.

"Me as well, as it truly will be a new era of compassion on the earth—a new consciousness," Sombra signed.

They remained there in silence until darkness swept over them like a comforting black velvet presence and they nodded off, exhausted yet secure in the warm embrace of Mother Earth and each other, confident in the knowledge that they were being cared for and protected.

On waking the following morning, Adan remembered having another *remembering session* while in a dream state that night before.

"Sombra, wake up! I had another *remembering session* last night involving my dear friend Marcia, who offered Source in Silence healing sessions before the near miss. You were only a puppy when I first met her. I saw her come up to me at a party and said, 'I know you are messing with everyone, but I know you really do see energy because I do also. I channel healing energy in silence.'

"I had been remarking to my friends that I could see that they were losing energy from particular points on their body. I would point them out, and each person would respond with a loud, 'Yes, how could you know my neck is aching, or my sciatica is acting up, or I have a pulled muscle, or my tooth hurts.' It wasn't long before everyone was lining up in front of me and asking what I saw on them. I could really see their energy as if it were leaking at those particular points on their bodies. I was having a great time.

"The scene changed to her office, where I'd agreed to her offer to engage me in a session with her. I heard a bell ring three times, she walked in, and I stood facing her, not two feet apart. As soon as we made eye contact, I saw us being transported side by side out of that room into space—through our solar system, past Jupiter with its one red eye, past the rings of Saturn, and through deep space, full of galaxies, stars, and nebulae. We came to rest within a huge, dimly lit triangular cavern full of flat outcroppings of what looked like pinkish-red shale or flagstone. High above us and to my right stood a being with a long white beard, wearing a long white robe, and holding a long staff with a silver ankh at a forty-five-degree angle at its tip. Seeing us, the being lifted his staff, and a beam of golden energy emanating from the point high above us reflected off the ankh toward us, completely surrounding us.

"As the beam of energy seemed to retreat to its source, we began our journey through space, retracing exactly our path until we returned to our places in her office. In silence, she turned from me and went to the room from which she had entered. After a few moments, she returned with two cups of tea, and I thanked her. I did not share my experience of what had happened with her. She then said she normally did not discuss the content of a session to remain a pure channel and ordinarily could not remember any of it anyway, but in this case, she could not remain quiet. She then described in full detail exactly what I also had experienced and said nothing like that had ever happened to her before with a client.

"I then came out of the *remembering session* in my dream knowing that we were connected to one another somehow through extraterrestrials. Amazing, isn't it, Sombra?"

16

"Companion" and Missing Time

"We're ready now, Sombra. Our contingency plans are in place in case anyone or anything tries to come get us—even though our plans may consist of, at most an inner, rather than an outer, reality, at least we've got something in place until we acquire more information on our intruders."

Sombra signed, "Remember, manifestation on the outside always begins with the inside," as Adan readied himself for his *remembering session.*

Slowly, he began to drift back, backward in time, softly carried by the events of his life. And once again, he felt as if he were being pulled by a ball of string being unraveled in the opposite direction.

There was a slight difference, thought Adan, between this particular transition to the past and the others. He felt a keenness to his senses—a stronger, more intense focus that he attributed to a more profound centeredness because of the planet's restoration processes. He hoped that this would help his remembering.

He felt himself gliding slowly to a halt, much like a parachute diver approaching the ground, he thought, as he entered a scene in which his younger self was at the wheel of his old forest-green Volvo sedan. He was fidgeting in his seat and glancing at his watch while remarking, "Five-thirty! I should've never drunk that large diet soda when I stopped to get gas. I should know better when having to drive fifty-five for over two hours to get home!"

Adan remembered the statement to mean that he was driving home to Tesuque after working at the Residential Treatment Center in Albuquerque's South Valley and had stopped for fuel for his car after work, as was his custom. But, apparently, this time he had forgotten how quickly a large drink becomes a full bladder needing to be emptied over the course of seventy-two miles in heavy traffic at fifty-five miles an hour during rush hour.

The car sped onto the bumpy dirt road leading up Cerro de Palomas to his driveway. He turned right into the parking space above the steps leading to the casita across the yard from his home; now desperate to use the restroom, he brought his car to an abrupt stop and simultaneously turned off the ignition, grabbed his keys, engaged the parking brake, released his seatbelt, and happened to glance out the front windshield to an awesome sight.

"Whoa! Look at that!"

Suddenly and instantaneously, the scene became night, and Adan was outside in darkness watching his younger self mumbling in awe as he calmly locked the car door, briefcase in his left hand and rechargeable flashlight and car keys in the other.

"Hmm, that was strange," he said, pausing momentarily and staring blankly at the starlit sky before walking slowly across the parking lot through the gate up the steps to his home.

What a curious sight, thought Adan. One moment it was daylight and the next moment it was night, after seeing, for a split second, what seemed to be a tall entity in a grayish jumpsuit with an oblong head and two arms and two legs. What's more, he also observed that the flashlight was not turned on; that his younger self didn't seem to notice or, if he did, he didn't seem to care; and that he no longer expressed the urge to pee. Curious, indeed.

Adan surmised that the quick switch from day to night was not because of a fault in his remembering but, rather, that he, in fact, was witnessing the memory exactly as it had taken place those many years before. And he knew not to be concerned because he had come to trust his remembering process to give him whatever information it was that he needed and in the manner best suited for him to receive it.

He watched as his younger self entered the house, set his briefcase in the consulting room, and proceeded to reposition the flashlight on the recharger cradle on the windowsill in his bedroom without so much as a second thought. It was obvious to Adan that the flashlight had not been intended to be used for the benefit of his younger self, and what's more, he noticed that it was not in the car during the drive from Albuquerque.

Adan also thought it most curious that this younger self did not rush to use the bathroom. Instead, he observed him, quite calmly, call out to Sombra and proceed out the back door and up the hill to his parents' house.

"Hi, Sombra! Did you miss me?" his younger self said, opening the screen door.

"Where have you been?" his agitated mother interjected with a hint of frustration. "Your dog's been going crazy, barking all evening waiting for you."

"All evening?" He looked puzzled as he petted his puppy. "I've been at work like usual."

"But where have you been since work?" his father asked in Spanish. "Your mother was getting worried; you're late."

16—"Companion" and Missing Time

"Worried? I got off at three thirty, stopped for gas, and here I am. And what do you mean 'since work'? It was going on five thirty-five when I drove up, and here I am."

"But where have you been?" his father repeated, again in Spanish. "Look at the clock." His father took him by the arm to the metal sun clock on the wall beside the ornate wood-burning stove.

Adan's younger self stared at the clock, which showed the time to be eight forty, for what seemed to be an eternity. They had been arguing back and forth for five minutes.

"Are you okay?" his parents asked simultaneously in English and Spanish, looking more concerned than angry.

"Yeah, but it can't be eight forty. I swear it was five thirty when I drove in and came right here. But I did see something strange leaning against the wall of the casita when I drove in, and this is what it looked like."

He sketched the image of the entity on his pocket-sized notebook while trying to explain to his parents that all he could remember was driving in at five thirty and seeing the entity in broad daylight. Now it was three hours later and dark when he walked into his parents' house.

The scene now changed to daylight as Adan found himself overlooking the parking area from above. The entity could be seen leaning against the casita with its right arm while holding its head with its left arm. His younger self, once again, was turning off the ignition, engaging the parking brake, and glancing out the front windshield in awe before slowly getting out of the car and standing motionlessly after taking a few steps.

There it was, facing him in broad daylight in a one-piece silver-gray jumpsuit, with its legs slightly bent and still towering over him at a height of about eight plus feet. Its long, gloved toes gave it an appearance of walking on another set of hands while holding up its narrow form. One arm extended out in a manner of leaning, tentatively, against the wall of the casita with five, long, bony fingers. The other arm, elevated sharply and bent at the elbow, held a tenuous position with two of its five, long fingers against its horizontally egg-shaped, metallic helmet completely covering its head. It seemed to be in trouble as it stood in silence on the narrow, cement sidewalk surrounding the house

Adan thought the two sets of two rows of circular perforations, one set for each eye, with two long rows extending the full length of a mouth area on an otherwise smooth surface, gave it an expressionless and ominous appearance, strangely reminiscent of the humanoid alien *Klaatu* in the 1951 classic science-fiction film *The Day the Earth Stood Still*.

16—"Companion" and Missing Time

After a while, something curious began to unfold. The entity, still touching its helmet with its upraised arm, began waving its fingers in a type of greeting. Seeing this, young Adan seemed to change, losing all fear, and repeated the gesture as he moved toward the entity with a familiarity suggestive of a child seeing his mentor after a long absence. Both used this method to communicate without speaking, as their conversation was being expressed as thoughts and in a type of sign language, the same one Sombra learned from Adan only recently.

"It's good to see you, again," the entity said in a warm but commanding tone.

"Companion, I've missed you, sir."

Hearing this, Adan realized that it was the implant that had figured in the memory of his meeting with Krystela, that both were utilizing it to converse with one another. As they spoke, the entity communicated its need for young Adan for help getting back to its ship, located up the arroyo in the foothills of the Sangre de Cristo Mountains. Part of the journey would have to be made on foot, and there would also be a need for light, so he was directed to retrieve the rechargeable flashlight from his bedroom after finally using the restroom. He then helped the entity into the car with some difficulty but with extraordinary care.

He then drove up the arroyo as far as he could go and set out on foot while gently supporting Companion, who acted as his guide. Because it was still daylight, there was no use for the flashlight on their way to the craft. They hardly spoke, other than young Adan warmly asking how Companion was doing over the rough terrain or warning him to watch his step as they walked. It was obvious that they had a special, friendly, and close, caring relationship that had not changed and that they had only developed an unspoken intimacy over time.

Adan marveled as he remembered the details of that encounter. Upon arriving at the M-shaped craft, the visibly weakened Companion used the flashlight to signal photo-sensitive panels to open an entrance for them. Once inside, Companion took off his space helmet, to the hissing of venting gases; ingested what seemed like a medication; and lay down to rest for a while in a recliner shaped to the contour and height of his body.

He explained that he was in need because one of his engines had failed, and he had had a rough landing the night before, reminiscent of the Roswell incident. He, then, had gone to find Adan to seek his help in repairing the craft. But what he hadn't counted on was the severe aftereffects of not spending enough time decelerating from what he termed a "hypermagnetic drive." Companion said

16—"Companion" and Missing Time

that it caused a magnetic field imbalance in his body analogous to what human deep-sea divers described as the "bends" or high-altitude pilots experienced as "aeroembolism."

Adan was surprised as his memory unfolded, reminding him of how he had been befriended as a child by this "Companion," who had been assigned to Adan and had visited him throughout his life. It was as if this information had been with him all the time, much like how the information in a dream is with a person even though the actual dream may become irretrievable.

After a short rest, Companion instructed young Adan on how to help him by placing his hands between alternating magnetic field poles. It seemed that the craft was a type of extension of Companion's magnetic field that needed to be "modulated," much like a radio frequency. But because of Companion's imbalance, he needed young Adan's similar genetic magnetic field to help restore the craft as well as Companion's health. Over time, a "harmonic magnetic field convergence" had genetically developed, imbued, and was now shared between them.

With Adan's help, after a time, the craft and Companion were now restored. Young Adan was told that Companion would continue to monitor his development and would, in the not-too-distant future, return to retrieve

Adan for his mission. Companion now transported him back through the hills and down the arroyo to the car as young Adan freely accepted a "false memory lapse" to account for the time spent helping Companion. He would initiate the "lapse" himself upon arriving at his destination to not disrupt the future unfolding of his natural development. This was accomplished by merely pressing twice on the implant on his left temple.

The scene began to fade as young Adan was placed contentedly in the darkness beside his car while Companion, who watched from the craft, hovered over-head. Time seemed to stop in those few moments as a feeling of profound peace and wonder replaced the image of young Adan standing silent with fingers outstretched in the same gentle gesture of greeting that each had made earlier when meeting and recognizing each other. It was as if the feeling bridged time, place, distance, and difference, reaching across the cosmos and joining all creation in the universe in a single rhythm of peace, love, understanding, and connection.

"I will be with you always," Companion said as the scene faded completely.

17

STAR CHILD

Adan, savoring the moment and touched by his own remembering, floated in the darkness and starlight, enveloped by feelings of joining and communion for what seemed like an eternity before returning to the present. It was all beginning to come together in a tight mosaic of clarity. Marveling at how it all was beginning to make sense to him, he understood that his remembering was necessary for bringing fully to consciousness that which he already had been living with his faithful friend. Sombra, who had listened attentively and gathered as much information as he could from every *remembering session,* was waiting by his side.

"Sombra! I think I've remembered it all. I'm now understanding more and more of the connections between my UFO experiences, the near miss and Earth's changes. Companion taught it all to me a long time ago, but it had to remain part of my unconscious until I could grow to accept it by living it so I could understand fully. Let me share with you what I now remember."

He proceeded to explain his involvement with Companion and the extraterrestrials, which began for him before he was born, as Sombra sat up and listened with wide-eyed interest.

"To begin with, the extraterrestrials from the planet of the Red Crystal in the Pleiades star cluster had been involved in their own internal power struggles for much of their evolution. Fearing ultimate annihilation of their species, a group of *Searchers*, elite intergalactic scientific explorers, from the Red Crystal planet set out on a voyage to preserve their race by introducing their own DNA into the evolution of any compatible life-forms in the multiverse.

"Do you remember the 'new age' movement in the 1990s? They had long maintained that many star groups had, in fact, joined themselves genetically to humans."

"So they were correct," Sombra signed.

"Yes, but that's not all. The *Searchers* had discovered the Earth among other planets in our galaxy and studied its inhabitants for many years because they had long since recognized the human race as most DNA compatible with their own species. A decision was reached to introduce

17—STAR CHILD

their DNA material, but because humans were less evolved than the Pleiadeans at the time, human DNA was altered to accept its Pleiadean counterpart. In a like manner, the Pleiadean DNA was also altered to lie dormant until humans were evolved enough to sustain it. It then would begin to manifest slowly in certain children over Earth's evolution, who afterward were referred to by the Pleiadeans as Star Children."

Sombra's ears perked up higher and his eyes widened at each startling piece of new information.

"But both sets of DNA began to interact with one another almost immediately, albeit imperceptibly and slowly began to alter their human hosts. As a result, the original twelve human strands and the sixty-four Pleiadean strands combined into two very complex strands of DNA to form the present double helix in humans.

"Also, many other earth species were experimented on, with the splicing of Pleiadean DNA onto their own, resulting in the same double helix, so common among Earth's inhabitants.

"It's also interesting to note, that while all shared the same double helix as a result of the joining of DNA, the actual evolved manifestation of Pleiadean genetic material only came about in a very small minority of earthlings recognized as Indigo Children and then as Crystal Children by humans.

"Indigo Children were highly technical, lacking emotional complexity, and then they evolved into Crystal Children exhibiting a complex blend of technical expertise and emotional empathy."

"Fascinating!" Sombra signed.

"Meanwhile, the Pleiadeans evolved out of their violent and warlike culture into a more complex, spiritual species, thus preserving themselves from extinction. They even regretted the fact of their interference in the evolution of all Earth's inhabitants by their experimentation and genetic engineering.

"Consequently, Earth began to be continuously monitored and visited periodically by other star groups with its human inhabitants scrutinized for overt signs of its hybrid Pleiadean–human evolution. This process of examination continued until it was noticed that only a certain few of the human children began appearing randomly and showing obvious signs of the Pleiadean DNA hybridization over Earth's evolutionary history. Some I read about were Akbar I, Lao Tzu, Wovoka, Socrates, Galileo, Rumi, Popé, Leonardo da Vinci, Kahlil Gibran, Princess Scheherazade, Alexander the Great, Gandhi, Einstein, Maria Tallchief, Mother Teresa of Calcutta, Hiawatha, and Sitting Bull. And

17—STAR CHILD

in my time, I also showed the signs of one of those hybrid Star Children."

"I knew it!" Sombra signed, his ears sticking up straight in awe.

"And so did other Earth inhabitants, like Koko the gorilla and now you also! The Earth changes only accelerated the process.

"As for Companion, as he came to be called, he had been sent to be the caretaker and tutor of some Earth Children in my time who were showing the evidence of their genetic origins beyond the earth. Companion would gather the Star Children on one ship during certain times in their development and test them and teach them. Afterward, each would be returned with a false memory, consciously oblivious to the visitation, so that each individual's conscious development would continue undisturbed."

"So that is why you remember and have had so many UFO and visitation experiences throughout your life," Sombra signed.

"Probably so, which also explains why I've always felt so different from my family and most other humans—I even used to tell everyone that I was exchanged at birth by being placed in a human body by aliens, but the technology was so primitive that my life-force constantly leaked," he said, chuckling. "My mother hated me saying that."

"Because, being a Star Child, you were trying to make conscious sense of it all, but it was the other way around. It was Companion who appeared to you-to teach you.

"And you, too, are a Star-Being. No other animal, myself included, has exhibited your rise in consciousness, your intellectual reasoning processes, or your level of empathy. All are related I believe, to the actualization of your Pleiadian genes; the changes to Earth only accelerated the process. It wasn't only human beings who were genetically engineered, remember?"

"I had often wondered why I developed such an extraordinary capacity. I thought it was merely a mutant phenomenon," Sombra signed.

"I really do believe that the Earth's changes were only the occasion, the spark as it were, to speed up the process, much like how the Pleiadeans use magnetic fields to traverse the universe. There seems to be a relationship between magnetic field processes and evolutionary development. At least that is what I've understood from my experience with Companion."

"And your Companion . . . will he ever be back?"

"Whoa, yes, he said so, but that's the strange part. At the end of my *remembering session*, as he was hovering

17—STAR CHILD

overhead and young Adan was gesturing farewell as the scene had faded, I heard him say, 'I will be with you always.' I felt great, totally connected—but something about those words."

"'I will be with you, always.' ... Did not your Jesus figure utter those same words to you when you were in high school?" Sombra signed.

"That's it! It's the same phrase! You don't suppose he was an alien? Wait, nah, the biblical Jesus never existed, only a collection of teachings."

"Well, maybe we can think more about that later. Yet, what was the rest of the phrase? "I will be . . . until . . ."

"'I will be with you until the consummation of the world,'" Adan interrupted.

"Ah yes, well, the world as we knew it has been consummated," Sombra signed. "Maybe we should expect a visit. After all, other groups seem to be here already."

"Maybe, but before we put out the welcome mat, we need to get some rest."

Agreeing, they walked to the couch. Sombra then caressed Adan's hair and softly hummed what seemed to be his interpretation of a lullaby as Adan curled up against him.

18

The Return

The sun shone brightly through the large skylights as a cool breeze from the open windows in the mall wound its way to the couch where Adan lay. Sombra, on the other hand, convinced that they were to be visited by Companion, had decided to begin preparations. He busied himself compiling the lists of questions they had agreed on based on all of Adan's *remembering sessions, as* well as adding a few of his own.

Especially intriguing to him were the religious experiences that needed explanation. The Jesus phrase, 'I will be with you always, until the consummation of the world,' continued to repeat itself in his mind. Sombra could not find a connection between Companion and that phrase which made any sense, other than the conclusion he had already come to that Companion would return at the dawning of the new Earth.

Just then, Sombra's ears perked up, and his attention was diverted to the ceiling as the silence was shattered with the sounds of whistling laser beams, explosions sparking in an orgasm of multi-colored metal and the low droning of the engines which caused enough vibration that the skylights and windows splintered, spewing glass everywhere. The building shook to its foundations, and pieces of the outside walls crumbled at the impact of what seemed to be stray fireballs.

Adan, who had been thrown from his couch, looked up in horror and watched in disbelief through the gaping space where the skylights had been only moments before.

"Look, Sombra! The UFO that looked like staples," he said, pointing.

Sombra could only point in the opposite direction of the sky at a saucer shape with a dome on top.

"They're firing at each other! Let's get out of here!"

Sombra stopped him in mid-panic and signed, "Where would we go? The only place more protected than this is probably a basement."

"A basement . . . oh . . . yeah, a basement—let's go! But do you have any idea which one is best? We don't want to be buried under debris!"

18—The Return

Sombra signed, "Follow me to the one underneath the grocery store. Remember? We spent time stocking it with essentials."

Recovering from his panic, Adan drew Sombra to himself, and both started out into the hallway, carefully, by crouching and walking closely against the walls of their quarters for protection. Sparks and debris fell sporadically as they tried to make their way to the other end of the mall amid the thunderous noise and crackling above them.

"It looks like it's too dangerous to try going through here," Adan said with a sudden frown of uneasiness. "What about going around the building through the outside?"

"Sure," Sombra signed with a nod. "But we must be very careful."

Amid the falling debris, the exploding light beams, and jarred nerves, they began their perilous trek around the building. Huddled together and walking slowly, Adan pointed to the field adjoining the parking lot. What looked like a group of alien intruders, clad in white from helmet to boot, were working a truncated pylon structure of white-metallic beams that had a type of cannon pointed skyward and sent intermittent bursts of beams of colored light into the sky.

"It's almost exactly like a dream I had as a young man," said Adan, clutching Sombra even tighter. "In my dream they overran the city of Santa Fe, giving the vicar, who was hiding in the basement of the Episcopal Church of the Holy Faith, a heart attack. It's just too fantastic to be really happening."

Sombra just shook his head in incredulous disappointment at what was happening.

They walked slowly past a group of beings holding ray guns without notice and turned a corner. All the while, beams of light shot in all directions in the sky with bursts of sparks spewing debris all around them in thunderous booms when meeting their target.

Suddenly, two of the intruders caught sight of them and began to give chase while firing their weapons at them as an apparent warning to stop. This only made Sombra and Adan run all the faster. They turned another corner, heading toward the grocery store basement with the intruders in pursuit. Looking ahead to another mall entrance, they came to an abrupt halt. Standing just ahead of them at the doorway was a familiar being, eight feet tall and touching the egg-shaped metallic space helmet with one hand and holding a square metallic device in the other. While gesturing the familiar greeting of years past with the

18—The Return

fingers against his head, Sombra and Adan also heard Companion ask them to come quickly and grab onto him.

Glancing at each other, they gestured hurriedly in a return greeting, rushed forward, and grabbed onto Companion. Instantly, they saw a ripple form in the air around them and felt a wave come over them as they disappeared into the space. At that moment, the intruders turned the corner and, seeing no one, came to a halt; they could only look at each other and at the mall entrance in apparent confusion.

Adan and Sombra found themselves alone with Companion. Still somewhat nervous and surprised, they were also relieved at having been retrieved from the intruders. Both were still clutching onto Companion.

"Are you all right, Sombra?" a breathless Adan asked. "I'd never forgive myself if anything ever happened to you."

Panting, Sombra nodded yes and signed, "Thank you," with his free paw.

"Where are we, Companion?" Adan asked, exchanging glances with Sombra.

"We are safe."

"But where?"

"Let us walk a little ways and sit down so that I may explain to you."

"It's not that Sombra and I are not grateful—we are. It's just that, after all we've been through, this latest turn of events is difficult to assimilate."

"Yes," Sombra signed. "And there are many questions that I would like to ask, if I may?"

I hope to answer all to your satisfaction, my little ones, but let us walk just a little farther," Companion said in a tone similar to Spock from the *Star Trek* TV series.

Adan found it interesting that Companion had understood and responded to Sombra's sign language. It was as if there was also a connection between Companion and Sombra. It would be something Adan would want to explore further when they got to their destination.

They walked until they arrived at the Companion's ship, which Adan thought looked much the same as he remembered it had those many years before. Companion opened a gangway out of the side of the ship and gestured for them to enter; they entered, and all of them sat.

"First, let me begin by saying that we are in an interdimensional space-time on your planet. Using this device, we have altered the magnetic fields around us and changed the physical characteristics of this area, allowing us to exist between dimensions of space and time in a fold. Einstein had also theorized that these folds in time and space could exist in this way. And no, Sombra, we are not responsible for the planetary changes that have taken place because of the shifting magnetic poles."

Sombra's ears perked up as he looked at Adan and signed, "How did he know that that is what I was thinking?"

Before Adan could utter a response, Companion responded tenderly, "You have an implant, much like Adan's, which allows me to communicate with you and allows you to communicate with me without speaking. This is how both of you heard me call you as you turned the corner while being pursued and how it seemed that I understood Sombra's sign language."

Sombra and Adan sat silently. Finally, Adan asked, "Who are those that are fighting, and why were they after us?"

"They are two factions of the same race from a neighboring planet in the Pleiades. As you remember, Adan, we evolved out of our violence, but those who could not accept peaceful coexistence were forced to leave. They formed alliances among themselves against others and left our star system in search of habitable planets from which to continue their existence."

"So they have been fighting ever since and now are taking advantage of our most recent planetary changes, what, in order to colonize this planet?" Adan said in a moment of anger.

"Yes and no. Competing factions have had their attention on this planet for a very long time—especially because of its Pleiadean connection. Now they seek to take advantage of the present circumstances and are willing to fight for control."

"And us?" Sombra signed. "How do we fit in?"

Just then, a combination growl and shriek from inside a corner of the ship interrupted their conversation. Startled, they all jumped and stumbled away from their places as Adan asked, "What was that?"

But before Companion could answer, a small, scruffy gray-and-white-haired head with a black button nose peered out of the darkness and looked around almost mechanically.

"Is that for real?" Adan chuckled, shaking himself off in an effort to calm himself.

"Oh, I almost forgot. Meet my companion. She is a twelve-year-old female of your species, Sombra—a canine miniature schnauzer. She was an unfortunate victim of this planet's ignorance, her former caretakers abandoning her as Earth's changes began."

"Where did you find her?" an inquisitive Sombra signed.

18—The Return

"At a caged facility for animals in Los Alamos. I was exploring the meson unit at the laboratory one night for radioactive materials that might escape into the environment once the changes to Earth began when I saw her shivering in the outside compartment of her cage. She was quite ill. So I whisked her into my ship to restore her health. I believed her to be about twelve of your Earth years of age."

"I do not understand how anyone could abandon a being after such a bond having been created. What's her name?" Adan asked sympathetically as he walked over and reached out to pet her.

"I believe the tag on her cell read 'Bon-Bon,' but I don't call her that. I named her after the flowers you gave me once when you visited my ship during one of my visits—Daisy."

Adan and Sombra could see the tenderness with which he treated Daisy. They also recognized how tired Companion had become when he asked to take a short rest period. So Sombra and Adan spent the rest of the afternoon walking with Daisy and relaxing in the warmth of each other's company.

19

The Mission

After a short walk and a long nap, Adan, Sombra, and Daisy returned to conversing with Companion.

Emerging from his living quarters and walking toward them Companion exclaimed proudly, "You both are very special! You showed signs of your Pleiadean and Earthly heritage from birth. You are the successful merging of our species that will ensure survival. And surviving the changes on this planet as advanced beings like yourselves, you are proof that our joined species will persevere."

"But are there no others like us?" Sombra signed.

"Yes, there are groups of survivors on this planet, but I have followed you both closely since birth—especially you, Adan. When we were together, I guided you with teachings, which were designed to help your development. And their practice allowed for the actualization of your potential with your consent, which you gave wholeheartedly at each face-to-face meeting over the years of your lifetime."

"And the reason being? Was not your species survival assured, once violence was no longer an issue?" Adan stared steadfastly at Companion.

"Yes." Companion now sat motionless. "But the issues now were your species and violence and guilt. We were ashamed by our interference and our unforeseen contribution to your violence, which we were afraid might destroy your species before having the opportunity to evolve out of it. So we decided to visit Earth's inhabitants periodically during their development, identifying potential Star Children to ensure ultimate survivability of the species and to help instill the futility of violence, amongst other more positive values in random others.

"And since your emergence, Adan, it was recognized that you showed a promising potential that was different from all others on the planet. That is why you were given special experiences to guide you in your development and to test you accordingly."

"And those experiences, tell me of them," Adan said, smiling gently,

"Yes, especially the religious ones," Sombra signed.

19—The Mission

"You, Adan, have inherent knowledge of all this that can be accessed through your remembering processes. You need only to remove the false memory overlaps which shield your consciousness, which I will instruct you how to do so. And you, Sombra, need to actualize that same remembering potential within you."

"But how?" both asked simultaneously.

"Let me help you remember—that you may release that which is within: that which is your destiny, and placed them in a trans state to direct them."

Companion waited for them to fully regain consciousness then stood and came to them with outstretched arms and, placing his hands upon the crowns of their heads, gently pressed alternately what seemed to be a code with his fingers. Adan and Sombra relaxed deeply into themselves and released all barriers as each traveled to his innermost being once again.

After removing his hands from their heads, Companion sat back and waited for Adan's and Sombra's return to consciousness while petting Daisy, who had jumped onto his lap. Slowly, both began to awaken to full awareness as Companion continued to speak.

"Adan, it was your strong spiritual connection that caught our attention. That is why we used so many of your Western civilization's religious images with which to guide you. And to not interrupt your development, yet allow for the building of a spiritual framework within you, we used holographic communication around the specific religious themes from your culture and family's religious belief system. And it did not matter that they were not real or nonexistent in terms of concrete, historical reality that you yourself concluded. The point was to develop a strong framework to contain your growing spiritual power.

"The first hologram was the Jesus image giving you the biblical message to tell your people that the end was near. In effect, a warning to guide your species to look inward, to listen with their hearts, to discern, reflect and change their lives by growth in integrity and love to survive the coming asteroid and Earth's changes, as you did.

"Next was the verbal holographic message through your implant about the great trial you were entering — which was about the struggle within yourself to recognize and grow beyond the cultural and societal limitations of all institutionalized spirituality-religion as practiced on your planet to fulfill your true being. In time you would have the choice to outgrow your religiosity and thus prove to be a true, universal spiritual leader or to retain your religiosity by becoming a leader of your own ego-making, like others in your world. This was the test.

19—The Mission

"We even tried to warn you by giving you a hint about the struggle you would face when we made the face of that archbishop grimace at you. But we had a few technical problems with the hologram that followed, which led to you to see that red sheet of energy emerge over you and the subsequent waking-nightmare images you experienced through your implant. We had planned actual images. We are fallible, after all."

"And the searing of the image of Jesus on the inside of the chalices?" Adan asked.

"Those, also, were of our making. In moments of stress they were sent to be recognized as archetypes of approval using the iconic image of a sacred heart because you embodied so much of that true spirit and you were having such difficulties at that time with the corrupt religious authority."

"And the earlier images?"

"The morphing hologram, which you correctly identified and called a SHIKARI, was an early attempt at capturing a being's stage of development. Only it was to happen when the being was in a sleep state. Unfortunately, you were not.

"And the UFO you consciously remembered as a spotlight and witnessed with your parents and uncle was a Searcher ship having engine trouble. Our ships tended to be inconspicuous, for the most part. And your uncle's presence was purely coincidental, although he was scrutinized, as were all those who were close to you who had some influence over your particular development."

"But why?"

"You see, our people have long awaited the appearance of a spiritual guide chosen to help us with the next step in our spiritual development. That being is to be charged with the mission of bringing together all our species who separated and went their different ways into the stars. It was also prophesied that the being would be a hybrid Pleiadean from beyond our star system accompanied by other hybrid Pleiadeans of a species different from his own."

"And the task of finding and joining spiritually, of our many species, is necessary for our entering the next phase in our evolution and continuing our growth and development.

"That is why it was Hermes, the messenger god of the ancient Greeks, who appeared to you among the lilac bushes in your front yard. Remember, he was clad in only a laurel leaf belt around his waist, barefoot with a wing growing out of the ankle of each foot and he wore a winged laurel leaf crown around the curly locks of hair on his head. He smiled, as he lay on his side with his chin resting on the

19—The Mission

palm of his hand, in acknowledgement of your ability to recognize and traverse the various phases of spiritual development and your empathic ability to guide others through theirs.

"Yes, Sombra. We believe that person to be Adan accompanied by species like yourself who were fulfilling their evolutionary potential. You see, you have been his guide as were your ancestors early in your species evolution on this planet. And yes, this is why you both were being pursued. If caught, you could be exploited and used to exercise control over the other groups."

"So I have come one last time, on behalf of all our joined species, to ask if you would take your place, freely, among the star systems of our many peoples in the multi-verse as a Spiritual Guide."

Adan and Sombra were surprised at the abruptness with which this last piece of information was shared with them and asked for time to process it all. Companion, for his part, asked that they reflect on his request, look inward, and listen to their hearts where their answer was to be found. Companion then left them in silent meditation for some time as they allowed their hearts to speak.

Nodding their assent, by bowing, and upon joining their hands in the Namaste gesture, they accepted. Adan asked, "And what of our planet and those who wish to exploit the remaining inhabitants? What will become of them?"

"Once you have been taught and taken your rightful place amongst the many on the planet of the Red Crystal, we will accompany your return so that you may assume your duties from Earth. In the meantime, observers from our people in your galaxy will be dispatched to monitor and hold this planet as a neutral zone until your return, and you and the remaining survivors will decide the direction that your world is to take. I am told that the survivors on your planet are already being contacted, are being cared for, and are being given an introduction to our species."

Companion then asked Adan to remember the energy session he had had with his friend Marcia in those months leading up to the near miss.

"You remember how awed you were to travel through your solar system and out through your galaxy into space, ending up within that pyramid structure on that faraway planet? We used Marcia's openness to Source to channel that visit to the home planet of your ancient Egyptians' gods. You 'both' were transported to that planet to be imbued with the healing energy needed for the challenges to come. Her surprise was that of being taken along with you. She was only familiar with being the channel, not with also being a subject of a session for someone else. She

19—The Mission

continues to prepare and teach those survivors until your return. And yes, her little companions, Magic and Love, are with her.

"Adan, you are to be taken back to that planet for further spiritual training with the same elder who channeled that energy during that visit. He will guide you through the discipline necessary to continue your journey and prepare you for further spiritual growth and your new responsibilities.

"And, Sombra, you have now achieved that level of awareness necessitating resources that can only be found on what is commonly referred to as the 'Dog Star' star system, Sirius. There you will continue your training and evolution, along with Daisy, Prince BeBe al Kahlil, Princess Waggles Scheherazade, Lucy, Dusty, and Shorty, who all have been Adan's companions before you.

"And, Adan, that feathered being Princess Waggles led you to before her passing was the Egyptian goddess Ma'at in Pueblo Indian form. In fact, it was a sign that Princess is an enlightened being of pure Love embodying truth, balance, and harmony achieved long before the changes to Earth and who was to be taken directly to Sirius. She awaits you there with all your other canine companions, and at the appointed time, you are to join them there after your mission is fulfilled.

"Presently, another companion has chosen you to accompany you during this next phase of your evolution. Recall that she has begun calling out to you by projecting her image into your consciousness."

"But I thought it was only a waking dream or a hallucination I had earlier because of what we had just been through," a teary Adan responded. "But I did find it strange, even for me, that I also heard a female voice accompany the image in my mind. And it said, 'You need to adopt me. I am the one you need to adopt for your journey.' And her name is Gypsy Blu-Belle," Adan added matter-of-factly.

"She will join us during our journey after you and Sombra have had time to discuss, adjust, and accept what your new circumstances will entail," Companion said.

With that having been said, Companion placed a silver bracelet on Adan's right wrist and a silver collar around Sombra's neck as symbols of their duty. It was also a holographic protection and a communication and tracking device. Then they took their places in the ship next to Daisy and Companion, left that interdimensional space and continued their journey to the stars.

~ The End or a New Beginning ~

www.ingramcontent.com/pod-product-compliance
Lightning Source LLC
Chambersburg PA
CBHW070601010526
44118CB00012B/1403